D1252153

The Wrong Word Dictionary

RICHMOND HILL
PUBLIC LIBRARY

FEB 1 4 2012

CENTRAL LIBRARY
905-884-9288

BOOK SOLD
NO LONGER R.H.P.L.
PROPERTY

Also by Dave Dowling

The Dictionary of Worthless Words
Images of Steve Reeves
Steve Reeves: His Legacy in Films

BOOK SOLD
NO LONGER R.H.P.L.
PROPERTY

The Wrong Word Dictionary

2,500 Most Commonly Confused Words

Dave Dowling

2nd Edition

Marion Street Press
Portland, Oregon

Published by Marion Street Press
4207 S.E. Woodstock Blvd. # 168
Portland, OR 97206-6267
USA
http://www.marionstreetpress.com/

Orders and review copies: 800-888-4741

Copyright © 2011 by Dave Dowling
All rights reserved.
No part of this book may be reproduced or transmitted in any form
or by any means, graphic, electronic, or mechanical, including
photocopying, recording, taping or by any information storage
or retrieval system, without the permission in writing from the
publisher.

Printed in the United States of America
ISBN 978-1-933338-92-7

Library of Congress Cataloging-in-Publication Data

Dowling, Dave.
  The wrong word dictionary : 2,500 commonly confused words /
Dave Dowling. — 2nd ed.
      p. cm.
  ISBN 978-1-933338-92-7 (pbk.)
  1. English language—Usage—Dictionaries. 2. English language—
Errors of usage—Dictionaries. I. Title.
  PE1464.D69 2011
  423'.1--dc23

                                                2011026735

RICHMOND HILL
PUBLIC LIBRARY

FEB 1 4 2012

CENTRAL LIBRARY
905-384-9288

To my wonderful son Tim

Preface

"The difference between the almost right word and the right word is really a large matter—'tis the difference between the lightning-bug and the lightning."—Mark Twain

Unlike math and science, writing has very few absolutes. To that end, we're faced with making choices, and many times those choices are word choices. Since I began teaching technical and business writing in industry years ago, one lesson never grew old—an exercise on when to write the right word. Many writers confuse *complement* when they mean *compliment*, *compose* when they mean *comprise*, or *assume* when they mean *presume*. And hundreds of other mistaken word identities also exist. This quick reference aims to filter this confusion of words. Remember, writing is much easier to comprehend when the noise around it is eliminated.

Though totally not inclusive of all word pair mistakes, this book speaks to the common word choices that challenge us daily. This new edition consists of more than 1,200 entries and the meanings of over 2,500 individual words or phrases. Much of the content is based on word problems I've witnessed during my 30 years of business writing as well as the misuse commonly found in the online and print media.

The basic sound-alike words such as *to*, *too*, and *two,* or *here* and *hear* are not within these pages. But you will find other sound-alike words and basic pronoun possessives (*their*, *they're*, *there*, *who's* and *whose*, and *you're* and *your)* because they still give us problems. I've tried to eliminate obvious synonyms *(simultaneous* vs. *concurrently, rare* vs. *scarce*, etc.) and include just word pairs where the word distinction is still important yet challenging.

Note that a few entries may seem trivial and others may seem obscure or obsolete. Still other entries may show word confusion caused only by the subtle misspelling of a word (*spade* vs. *spaded*, *cite* vs. *site*). But overall you'll find it a good mix of problem words (*among* vs. *between, flounder* vs. *founder*, *blatant* vs. *flagrant)*.

Also included are a few notes on phrases that often lead to problem writing (*between you and I*, *one of the only,* and others).

For each entry in this reference, the difference between the words is explained, and in most cases, a short and simple sentence example showing the correct usage is provided. The word definitions provided are intended strictly as aids and not dictionary definitions. They should help you differentiate between the words. Current dictionaries, popular writing books, and reputable style guides were among the many resources consulted for this book. The word list is arranged alphabetically according to the first word in the set.

In addition to this reference, keep a current dictionary, thesaurus, and grammar book handy to guide all your writing and editing. And refer to those resources as well whenever you doubt the appropriateness of a word or phrase.

Always think about the words you use. Accuracy in word choice is a key to effective communication. In your daily writing, try to make sure you apply the *right word* for the *right meaning*. By doing so, its effect can affect your writing in a positive way.

Dave Dowling
Saratoga Springs, NY

Acknowledgments

This book would not have materialized without the sincere encouragement of my friend and former co-worker, Harry Dracon. After reading my weekly word tips on the company's intranet site, Harry strongly urged me to expand this idea into a book. I was reluctant at first because I doubted an audience existed for such a topic. I was wrong, and today I'm certainly glad I listened to a friend. Thank you, Harry, for all your inspiration, belief, and support. You were right to push me in this right word direction.

Whether it was ideas, constructive criticism, or encouragement when this project was in its online infancy, I must thank one person in particular who influenced me on this word journey. I'm particularly grateful to Robert Hartwell Fiske for all his professional advice and expertise. Thanks, Robert, for your generous time, and thanks for being there when I needed your expert editorial skills and guidance. I'm proud to know you and proud to be a part of your writing world.

I am also grateful to the many readers of the First Edition who sent in several ideas and comments. Thanks to your excellent feedback, I included many of those suggestions in this Second Edition. I'm sure many people will benefit thanks to you.

Finally, a heartfelt thanks goes to my son, Tim. Following in the footsteps of his late mother (and my late wife Mary), Tim encouraged me to pursue my writing interests, chase my dreams, and keep taking one step forward in anything I do. It's that spirit of optimism that will always keep me going. Thanks Tim and may God always bless you. You're my best critic and the joy in my life. I am so proud of your achievements in life, and so proud to call you my son.

The
Wrong
Word
Dictionary

A

"By words the mind is excited and the spirit elated."—Aristophanes

A hold, Ahold

Ahold is not a word. **A hold** is standard English.
*I prefer e-mail, but another way to get **a hold** of me is by phone.*

À la mode, Alamode

À la mode refers to being served with ice cream.
*The restaurant served pie **à la mode** with every meal.*

Alamode refers to a thin silk usually found in scarfs and hoods.
*She complemented her winter outfit with a black **alamode** scarf.*

A long way, A long ways

A long way is the correct phrase.
*If you become bilingual, your career can go **a long way**.*

A lot, Allot, Alot

A lot is always two words.
***A lot** of people today are doing business on the Internet.*

Allot means to allocate or share something.
*The education budget **allots** money for reading programs.*

Alot is not a word.

A part, Apart

A part refers to the union of something.
*Volunteering at the hospital has become **a part** of her routine.*

Apart refers to a separation in place, position, or time.
*If anything sets her **apart**, it's her volunteer work at the hospital.*

A ways

Incorrect phrase. The article **a** is singular; therefore, the word following **a** must also be singular (**way**).
*The Town Square Mall is **a** little **way** down the parkway.*

A while, Awhile

A while, a noun phrase, is used as the object of the prepositions *for* and *in*.
*Tom and Linda have decided to stay for **a while** in Otego.*
*In **a while**, Tom and Linda leave Otego for good.*

Awhile is an adverb that means for a time.
*Tom and Linda are deciding whether to stay **awhile** in Otego.*

Abbreviation, Acronym, Initialism

An **abbreviation** is a shortened word form of a word or phrase that cannot be pronounced as another word (Dept., Prof. Mgr., etc.). An **acronym** is a group of initials that can be pronounced as a word (radar, scuba, sonar, etc). An **initialism** is a group of initials that cannot be pronounced as a word (FBI, HTML, IRA, etc.).

Aberrant, Abhorrent

Aberrant means unusual or away from the norm.
*A complaint was filed concerning their **aberrant** behavior.*

Abhorrent means to detest something.
*People would find this material obscene and **abhorrent**.*

Abdicate, Abrogate, Arrogate

Abdicate means to give up, relinquish power, or renounce formally.
*By leaving the job, did Paul **abdicate** his rights to a pension?*

Abrogate means to abolish, cancel, or revoke something.
*Why are the politicians seeking to **abrogate** the agreement?*

Arrogate means to take, claim, or assume without any right.
*He **arrogated** to himself what should be in the company charter.*

Ability, Capacity

Ability refers to the power to do something.
*Some vitamins are said to have the **ability** to prevent colds.*

Capacity refers to the ability to hold or contain something.
*Madison Square Garden has a **capacity** of 20,000 seats.*

Abjure, Adjure

Abjure means to recant, renounce, or repudiate something.
*To the council's surprise, he **abjures** all rights to his citizenship.*

Adjure means to appeal, entreat, or order something.
*The club **adjures** its members to show respect at all times.*

Abnormal, Subnormal

Abnormal means deviating from the average.
*Her **abnormal** powers of concentration enable her to score well.*

Subnormal means less than normal or below the average.
*His SAT scores are **subnormal** and not as high as he expected.*

About, Approximately, Around

About refers to a rough estimate.
*We are **about** halfway through the class and enjoying it.*

Approximately refers to near accuracy.
*The college currently enrolls **approximately** 4,000 students.*

Around refers to a physical proximity or surrounding.
*We'll look for you **around** the front of the building.*

Abridged, Expurgated, Unabridged

Unabridged means in its full length or original content. **Abridged** means abbreviated or condensed. **Expurgated** means objectionable material has been removed.

Abstemious, Abstinent

Abstemious means eating or drinking in moderation.
*Barb's **abstemious** habits probably ensure her a longer life.*

Abstinent means abstaining from something (food, drink, etc.).
*The young men pledge to remain **abstinent** until age 21.*

Abstractedly, Abstractly

Abstractedly means not paying attention, preoccupied, or removed.
*He sat through the lecture gazing **abstractedly** out the window.*

Abstractly means hard to understand or unspecific.
*Without pictures, he could only **abstractly** describe the tool.*

Abstruse, Obtuse

Abstruse means complex, deep, or difficult to understand.
*To the average person, Einstein's theory of relativity is **abstruse**.*

Obtuse means dull witted, not too sharp, or slow to understand.
*Sorry if I'm being **obtuse**, but I do not understand the point.*

Abundant, Fulsome

Abundant refers to something profuse or of great quantity.
*She received **abundant** praise for her work with the deaf.*

Fulsome refers to something so excessive it causes offense or disgust.
*Unfortunately, the host gave the speaker a **fulsome** introduction.*

Abuse, Misuse

Abuse means to use something badly or wrongly.
*I hope Frank doesn't **abuse** the new car his parents bought him.*

Misuse means to use something for which it was not intended.
*The students often **misuse** the school computers to play games.*

Accede, Concede, Exceed

Accede means to take a position of authority or to yield.
*He may **accede** to the throne, but only after taking the oath.*
*I **accede** to your demands, as long as they are realistic.*

Concede means to accept reluctantly.
*Friends urged the candidate not to **concede** on election night.*

Exceed means to surpass.
*The product and service **exceed** our customer's expectations.*

Accent, Dialect

Accent usually describes how people pronounce words of a language different from their mother tongue. It reveals one's place of origin.
*Arnold Schwarzenegger speaks English with an Austrian **accent**.*

Dialect is usually spoken by people who live in a certain region of a country. **Dialects** have distinctive vocabulary, pronunciation, intonation, and grammar.
*She spoke the language in a regional **dialect**, which made it difficult to understand.*

Accept, Except

Accept means to admit, receive, or agree.
*I **accept** him to our organization with pleasure.*
*We **accept** your invitation to the ceremonies.*
*They **accept** the jury's verdict with no problem.*

Except as a preposition means other than.
*The student's grades are low in every subject **except** science.*

Except as a verb means to exclude something.
*If you **except** his math grades, Ryan has an impressive average.*

Access, Excess

Access refers to an increase, outburst, or the ability to get something.
*Their winnings at the casino gave them an **access** of wealth.*
*What started as a small dispute turned into an **access** of rage.*
*We give certain users **access** to the secure web site.*

Excess refers to an overindulgence or surplus.
*Betty has an **excess** of property she would like to sell.*
*At the picnic, a few employees ate to **excess**.*

Accessary, Accessory

Accessory is the preferred spelling, but either is acceptable.

Accessible, Assessable

Accessible means capable of being approached, influenced, obtained, or understood.

*She works for an **accessible** supervisor whom everyone likes.*
*His technologies make TV **accessible** for the disabled.*
*The information is **accessible** to a nontechnical audience.*

Assessable means capable of being evaluated.
*The assessor classifies every item of **assessable** property.*

*Sorry, we **accept** every card **except** Visa.*

Accident, Incident, Mishap

Accident refers to an unforeseen event (good or bad).
*George's call about the job opening was just a lucky **accident**.*
*A flawed design contributed to the Chernobyl **accident**.*

Incident refers to a minor or simple occurrence (good or bad).
*The entire **incident** was recorded on video.*

Mishap refers to a minor unfortunate occurrence.
*Though no one was hurt, a **mishap** occurred during the parade.*

Accidentally, Accidently

Accidentally is the preferred spelling.
*If you **accidentally** delete the file, it is possible to restore it.*

Acclamation, Acclimation

Acclamation refers to an oral vote or praise of some kind.
*The board passed by **acclamation** a motion to fund the plan.*
*The Honor Society appreciated the **acclamation** of the principal.*

Acclimation refers to adapting to a new climate or environment.
*Her **acclimation** to the cold weather took longer than expected.*

Accompanied by, Accompanied with

Accompanied by refers to people or animals.
*Everywhere the Queen goes, she is **accompanied by** the King.*

Accompanied with refers to objects.
*No photograph will be used that is not **accompanied with** the
release form.*

Accord, Accordance

Accord refers to an agreement or settlement.
*Congress arrived at a unanimous **accord** on the amendment.*

Accordance refers to conformity to regulations.
*My plan is in **accordance** with the Stock Exchange Regulations.*

Accuse, Allege

Accuse means to blame or charge someone with wrongdoing.
*No one **accuses** him of mishandling the funds.*

Allege means to claim something not yet proven.
*The investigator **alleges** the investors were tricked by a scam.*

Acetic, Aesthetic, Ascetic

Acetic refers to things having an acid characteristic.
*Because of its **acetic** taste, there's a chance the juice is old.*

Aesthetic refers to artistic or beautiful things.
*The architect designs buildings with **aesthetic** ideas in mind.*

Ascetic refers to a person austere in appearance, manner, or attitude.
*He lives an **ascetic** existence, supporting himself on a farm.*

Acidulous, Assiduous

Acidulous means tart or sour in taste or manner.
*Her **acidulous** wit makes her unpopular with some employees.*

Assiduous means diligent or persistent.
*He is **assiduous** in visiting the sick, wherever they live.*

Acknowledgment, Acknowledgement

Acknowledgment without the second e is preferred in American usage.
*Applicants are now receiving **acknowledgment** letters.*

Acme, Climax

Acme is the highest point.
*The **acme** of the classical piano recital was Sharon's song.*

Climax is the point of greatest intensity.
*The **climax** of the night's events is the colorful fireworks display.*

Acquaintance, Friend

An **acquaintance** is a person one knows. A **friend** is a person one knows, likes, and trusts.
*Joe is an example of an **acquaintance** who became a **friend**.*

Acquiesce in, Acquiesce to, Acquiesce with

Acquiesce means to consent or comply without protest. When **acquiesce** takes a preposition, it is usually **in**.
*His government can't **acquiesce in** the invasion of that country.*

Acquiesce with the preposition **to** is uncommon, but acceptable.
*Gracie, Audrey, and Patrick **acquiesced to** their parents' wishes.*

Acquiesced with is considered obsolete.

Acquitted from, Acquitted of

Acquitted of is the preferred phrase.
*The suspect is **acquitted of** all charges relating to the case.*

Acute, Chronic

Concerning physical condition:

Acute refers to an extremely severe or sharp condition.
*While playing basketball, he experienced **acute** stomach pain.*

Chronic refers to a lingering or prolonged condition.
*Through stretching exercises, one can relieve **chronic** back pain.*

Ad, Add

Ad is the shortened form of **ad**vertisement.
*We placed an **ad** in the classified section of Sunday's paper.*

Add means to total something or contribute to something.
*If we **add** every golf score, we played better than many teams.*
*Let's **add** more sugar to the lemonade.*

Ad hoc, Ad lib

Ad hoc refers to a specific purpose, case, or situation at hand.
*The committee was formed **ad hoc** to address the problem.*

Ad lib refers to something being spontaneous or unrestrained.
*Her impressive speech was 50% **ad lib** and 50% rehearsed.*

Ad nauseam, Ad nauseum

This much overused phrase is often spelled incorrectly as **ad nauseum**.

Adage, Axiom

Adage refers to a saying that has obtained acceptance.
*"Nothing ventured, nothing gained" is an **adage** many use.*

Axiom refers to a universally accepted rule or principle.
*This **axiom** is consistent with the rules of set theory.*

Adapt, Adept, Adopt

Adapt means to adjust, change, or make suitable.
*Christian **adapts** well to new working environments.*

Adept means to be skilled at something.
*Among other things, Frances is **adept** at shuffling cards.*

Adopt means to accept or to take as your own.
*Because of its merits, we shall **adopt** your proposal immediately.*
*Our son, who is now 18, was **adopted** 10 weeks after his birth.*

Addenda, Agenda

Addenda (plural) are additions to something.
*The **addenda** to the manual give the hardware requirements.*

Agenda is a schedule or a list of things to do.
*The **agenda** for this year's seminar is interesting and varied.*

Addition, Edition

Addition is something added.
*Jane and Kerry built an **addition** to their camp last summer.*

Edition is one complete issue of a publication.
*That story should be in the newspaper's latest **edition**.*

Adduce, Deduce, Deduct

Adduce means to cite as an example of proof in an argument.
*The attorneys did not try to **adduce** fresh evidence in the case.*

Deduce means to conclude from a rule, principle, or reasoning.
*Brian **deduced** from the laws of physics that the plane would fly.*

Deduct means to take away from.
*Some believe too many taxes are **deducted** from their wages.*

Adhere, Cohere

Adhere means to stick fast, to be devoted, or to carry out a plan.
*Using that glue, the wallpaper should **adhere** to the wall quickly.*
*They have **adhered** to that particular faith for many years.*
*We are taking your advice and **adhering** to the revised plan.*

Cohere means to hold together as part of the same thing.
*Generally, the film's subplots failed to **cohere**.*

Adherence, Adherents

Adherence refers to faithful commitment.
*His **adherence** to the corporation's goals was never in doubt.*

Adherents refer to advocates or supporters.
*Congress passed a law that pleased **adherents** of tax reform.*

Adieu, Ado, Á deux

Adieu means goodbye.
*Since joining the health club, Ty bid **adieu** to bad eating habits.*

Ado means bother, fuss, or trouble.
*"Husband, let's follow, to see the end of this **ado**."*—The Taming of the Shrew

Á deux means to involve two people in a private or intimate nature.
*The inn featured dining **à deux**, private porches, and cut flowers.*

Adjacent, Adjoining

Adjacent means next to but without physical contact.
*The basketball arena is directly **adjacent** to the team's hotel.*

Adjoining means having a common point of contact.
*The basketball team players have **adjoining** rooms in the hotel.*

Adjudicate, Arbitrate, Mediate

Adjudicate means to act as a judge in disputes.
*The department has jurisdiction to **adjudicate** all of the appeals.*

Arbitrate means to make a neutral judgment.
*Ken willingly agrees to **arbitrate** the contract dispute.*

Mediate means to bring parties together or reconcile differences.
*Ed is attempting to **mediate** the differences between the teams.*

Administer, Administrate

Administer is the proper verb form for *administration* or *administrator*.
*They wondered which lawyer would **administer** the estate.*

Adopted, Adoptive

Adopted refers to an accepted policy or responsibility.
*They **adopted** a new policy for handling delinquent accounts.*

Adoptive refers to adoption.
*Tim always felt content and happy with his **adoptive** parents.*

Advance, Advancement

Advance refers to improvement, movement, or progress.
*Her research resulted in an **advance** in molecular biology.*

Advancement refers to promotion.
*The fund is for the **advancement** of science and technology.*

Adverse, Averse

Adverse means difficult or unfavorable.
*The rule could have an **adverse** effect on our business.*

Averse means opposed to.
*The public relations director is **averse** to our business proposal.*

Adversity, Diversity

Adversity refers to affliction, hardship, or misfortune.
*After a year of financial **adversity**, the company rebounded well.*

Diversity refers to an assortment or a variety of things.
*To add **diversity** to your portfolio, consider this investment.*

Advert, Avert

Advert means to call attention to or refer to something.
*The speaker **adverted** to a point she had made earlier.*

Avert means to prevent or ward off something.
*To avoid any delays, management wants to **avert** a strike.*

Advise, Inform

Advise means to give advice, counsel, or suggestions.
*We will **advise** you on proper use of the new printer.*

Inform means to communicate information.
*The teachers will **inform** the students when the tests are graded.*

Advisedly, Intentionally

Advisedly means deliberately or with careful consideration.
*She chose her words to the media **advisedly**.*

Intentionally means with intent or purpose.
*The author **intentionally** left his phone off the hook.*

Adviser, Advisor

Adviser is the preferred spelling, but either is acceptable.

Aerial, Ariel

Aerial refers to a radio antenna or something else that reaches into the air.
*Before cable TV, many people put TV **aerials** on their roofs.*
***Aerial** photography is becoming one of her favorite pastimes.*

Ariel refers to a kind of gazelle or the brightest moon of Uranus.
*The **ariel** gazelle is under two feet tall and lives in the desert.*
*Much of **Ariel's** surface is pitted with craters.*

Aerie, Airy, Eerie

Aerie means nest.
*Have you ever been to the mountains and seen an eagle's **aerie**?*

Airy means breezy.
*The **airy** conditions at the New Jersey shore always keep us cool.*

Eerie means spooky.
*The séance we attended was an **eerie** experience for everybody.*

Aesthetic, Ascetic

Aesthetic refers to beauty or attractiveness.
*The new door will improve the **aesthetic** look of the house.*

Ascetic refers to avoiding pleasure or material comforts usually for religious reasons.
*He practices the doctrine that the **ascetic** life releases the soul.*

Affect, Effect

The verb **affect** means to influence or change.
*The moon and sun can **affect** the ocean's tides.*

The verb **effect** means to bring about or accomplish.
*The new CEO **effected** a few minor changes to the company.*

The noun **effect** means result.
*One **effect** of the drought was a skimpy corn crop.*

Memory hook: If you **affect** something, you can have an **effect** on it.

Affectation, Affection

Affectation refers to artificial, exaggerated, or false behavior.
*Forget the vocabulary **affectations**. We prefer plain language.*

Affection refers to fondness toward someone.
*The club has a deep **affection** and respect for that family.*

Affidavid, Affidavit

Affidavit is the correct word.

Affinity, Eternity, Infinity

Affinity means a close relationship or connection.
*The organization has a strong **affinity** for environmental issues.*

Eternity means unending time or forever.
*The pastor told the mourners that Jill would live an **eternity**.*

Infinity means unlimited quantity, space, or time.
*From the ground, that highway appears to go on for an **infinity**.*

Afflatus, Flatus

Afflatus refers to divine inspiration, and **flatus** refers to gas generated by the intestine.

Afflict, Inflict

Afflict means to cause suffering for someone or something.
*The disease first **afflicted** people who were not vaccinated.*

Inflict means to cause by aggressive action.
*The truck hit a parked car and **inflicted** severe damage to it.*

Affluent, Effluent

Affluent refers to the rich.
*Joan jokingly claims she is from an **affluent** background.*

Effluent refers to a river, stream, or lake that flows out.
*The farmer uses water from that **effluent** to water his garden.*

Aforementioned, Aforesaid

Aforementioned and **aforesaid**, meaning stated previously, should be restricted to legal writing.
*The judge indicated that the **aforementioned** would stand trial.*
*We hereby agree to the **aforesaid** usage of the information.*

Afterall, After all

After all is always two words.

Afterward, Afterwards

Afterward is preferred in American usage.

Aggravate, Irritate

Aggravate means to make something worse or more severe.
*Research shows that dust can **aggravate** lung problems.*

Irritate means to annoy.
*His management style **irritates** us.*
*Vitamin C, aspirin, and potassium can **irritate** the esophagus.*

Aggression, Egression

Aggression refers to hostility.
*The wild animals showed **aggression** toward their captors.*

Egression refers to the act of emerging.
*The hypnotist showed the man an **egression** into a future life.*

Agnostic, Atheist

An **agnostic** feels the existence of God cannot be proved or disproved. An **atheist** completely denies the existence of God.

Agree to, Agree with

Agree to means to concede to something.
*We hope the local officials can **agree to** a compromise this year.*

Agree with means to be in accord with something.
*Both parties **agree with** each other on the new spending plan.*

Agreeance, Agreement

Agreement is the preferred word. **Agreeance** is an obsolete word.

Aid, Aide

Aid refers to assistance.
*Animal **Aid** is one of the oldest animal rights groups in the world.*

Aide refers to a helper.
*The congressional **aide** says the senator is unavailable right now.*

Ailment, Aliment

Ailment refers to an illness.
*The skin **ailment** develops due to a bacterial infection.*

Aliment refers to supplying with sustenance, such as food or moral support.
*The law requires the family be supplied with different **aliments**.*

Aisle, Isle

Aisle is a passageway between seats, traffic, and other things.
*Two by two the wedding party marched down the **aisle**.*

Isle refers to a small island.
*The **Isle** of Wight was a famous 1970 concert venue in England.*

Ale, Lager

Both beverages are beer types. **Ale** is produced with a top-fermenting yeast, fermenting between 64 and 70 degrees. **Lager** is produced with a bottom-fermenting yeast, fermenting between 52 and 58 degrees. The difference in temperature can affect the taste. **Ales** typically are fruitier and **lagers** more crisp.

*The student was grateful for the **aid** the teacher's **aide** provided.*

All, alls

Use **all**, never **alls**.
*All (not **alls**) you hear them talk about are their careers.*

All I know is, Alls I know is

All I know is the correct phrase.
All I know is that the strict diet affected my cholesterol levels.

All kinds of

Avoid this awkward colloquialism. Use *many* or *much* instead.

All of a sudden, All of the sudden

All of a sudden is the correct phrase.
All of a sudden the media are covering that story.

All over, Allover

All over means finished or everywhere.
*The job of wallpapering the dining room was finally **all over**.*
*The paint spilled **all over** the floor.*

Allover means covering the entire surface of something.
*The wallpaper had an **allover** pattern of flowers and trees.*

All ready, Already

All ready means totally prepared.
*Steve tells us the system is **all ready** and available to use.*

Already means by this time or so soon.
*It was **already** noon before Steve could restart the system.*

All right, Alright

All right must always be two words. **Alright** is considered a nonstandard word. Avoid its use.
*It's certainly **all right** to be nervous before an important speech.*

All the farther, As far as

As far as is the preferred phrase.
*Is that **as far as** (not **all the farther**) you drove today?*

All together, Altogether

All together means in one complete group.
*The reports are **all together** on the conference room table.*

Altogether means completely, entirely, or totally.
*The presentation is **altogether** too long for next week's meeting.*

All ways, Always

All ways means by every way or method.
*Ensure they look **all ways** before crossing the intersection.*

Always means all the time or forever.
*We will **always** remember the good things they did for the poor.*

Allay, Alleviate, Assuage

Allay means to make less or to delete altogether.
*To **allay** the oil shortage, scientists are developing other fuels.*

Alleviate means to relieve something unpleasant or painful.
*Simple aspirin can quickly **alleviate** some of your discomfort.*

Assuage is similar in meaning but used for unpleasant situations.
*We tried to **assuage** the older man's fear of flying.*

Allegory, Analogy

Allegory is a literary or artistic work with a concealed meaning.
*The painting depicts an **allegory** of sin and redemption.*

Analogy is a comparison between different things that have a few things in common.
*They made an **analogy** between diet and high cholesterol.*

Allergenic, Allogeneic

Allergenic refers to a substance that can cause an allergy.
*He is testing the lotion to see if it causes **allergenic** problems.*

Allogeneic refers to belonging to the same species but being genetically different.
*The hospital offers **allogeneic** stem cell transplantation.*

Alliterate, Illiterate

Alliterate means to arrange words with a repeating initial consonant sound.
*Most tongue-twisters in Modern English **alliterate**. (**P**eter **P**iper **p**icked a **p**eck of **p**ickled **p**eppers.)*

Illiterate refers to the inability to read or write or the lack of knowledge in a certain subject.
*Sadly, 20 percent of their state's adults are **illiterate**.*
*Some of the students were computer **illiterate**.*

Allude, Elude, Refer

Allude means to hint or refer to indirectly.
*The memo did **allude** to past equipment failures and problems.*

Elude means to avoid or escape.
*After the hit, the base runner tried to **elude** the shortstop's tag.*

Refer means to make direct reference to something.
*If you have other questions, **refer** to the charts for more data.*

Allusion, Delusion, Illusion

Allusion is a reference to something.
*Emma makes **allusions** to her favorite books and authors.*

Delusion is a mistaken belief or opinion.
*He has a **delusion** that man never set foot on the moon.*

Illusion is a deceptive appearance.
*The optical **illusion** is actually an effect of perspective.*

Almost, Most

When you want to say *nearly all*, use **almost**.
*Kerry touches base with work **almost** (not **most**) every day of his vacation.*

Aloud, Out loud

Aloud is standard English. **Out loud** is considered colloquial.
*The teacher always enjoys reading **aloud** to the class.*

Altar, Alter

Altar refers to the platform at the front of a church or temple.
*They keep the daily prayer book on the church's **altar**.*

Alter means to change.
*The judge may **alter** her decision on cameras in the courtroom.*

Alteration, Altercation, Alternation

Alteration is a change.
*Some scientists believe gene **alteration** may raise cancer risk.*

Altercation is an argument, dispute, or fight.
*Play stopped because of an **altercation** in the outfield stands.*

Alternation is a constant back and forth change.
*The doctor experimented with the **alternation** of two remedies.*

Alterior, Ulterior

Ulterior, as in ***ulterior** motive*, is the correct word.

Alternate, Alternative

Alternate, as an adjective, means every other one. As a verb, it means to change from one to another.
*Every **alternate** Friday, Joe, Doug, and Eric meet for golf.*
*He **alternates** between his five wood and driver off the tee.*

An alternative is another option.
*The **alternative** is to leave early before the afternoon traffic.*

Although, Whereas

Although means in spite of the fact that.
***Although** your membership expired, we will honor your request.*

Whereas means to the contrary.
*The first lecture was boring, **whereas** the next one was fun.*

Alumna, Alumnus

Alumna is a former female student (plural is *alumnae*).
Alumnus is a former male student (plural is *alumni*).

Amateur, Novice

Amateur refers to someone who does an activity as a pastime.
*Arnold was an exceptional **amateur** before turning professional.*

A **novice** is a beginner.
*When it comes to playing golf or tennis, he is just a **novice**.*

Ambiguous, Ambivalent, Indifferent

Ambiguous means unclear or subject to interpretation.
*The candidate is so **ambiguous** that few know his platform.*

Ambivalent means having mixed feelings or being uncertain.
*He is **ambivalent** about returning to college for more courses.*

Indifferent means being apathetic or showing no concern.
*The legislature remains **indifferent** about building a new library.*

Amend, Emend

Amend means to add to or change.
*The surveys prove it; it's time to **amend** our society's charter.*

Emend means making changes or corrections, specifically to text.
*Before the next edition, the publisher wants to **emend** the book.*

Amiable, Amicable

Amiable means agreeable and easy to deal with, and is applied to a person.
*Bo is an **amiable** person with whom I enjoy playing golf.*

Amicable means good willed or friendly, and is used to describe relations between people or other entities.
*France maintains an **amicable** relationship with that country.*

Amiss, Remiss

Amiss means something is out of place.
*When we saw the broken glass, we knew something was **amiss**.*

Remiss means to be careless or neglect to do something.
*I was **remiss** in failing to mention other candidates.*

Ammunition, Munitions

Ammunition is anything discharged from a gun, plane, ship, etc.
*The **ammunition** supply depot is just a short distance away.*

Munitions is all war equipment.
*Reducing the toxicity of uranium depleted **munitions** is difficult.*

Among, Amongst

Among is preferred in American English.

Among, Between

Among is used for relationships involving more than two.
*The managers agree **among** themselves that the solution failed.*

Between is usually used for relationships involving only two, but may be used for more when the items are distinctly separate.
*Clean your cleats **between** the second and third innings.*
*Best golfer of the 1960s is **between** Arnold, Gary, and Jack.*
*The plane crash-landed in the field **between** the four houses.*

Amoral, Immoral

Amoral means without morality.
*They are known to be **amoral**, with no sense of right or wrong.*

Immoral means contrary to established moral standards.
*Though it is popular, some people may find the book **immoral**.*

Amount, Number

Amount refers to things that cannot be counted individually.
*Furnishing a new office requires a great **amount** of time.*

Number refers to countable things.
*The tenants bought a large **number** of PCs for the office.*

Ample, Enough

Ample means more than adequate in capacity, scope, or size.
*You have **ample** opportunity to talk with prospective clients.*

Enough means adequate or sufficient to satisfy a need.
*Make sure you have more than **enough** RAM to run the program.*

Amuse, Bemuse

Amuse means to entertain.
His jokes still amuse us, even though we've heard them all.

Bemuse means to bewilder, confuse, or stupefy.
The change in tactics appears to bemuse our opponents.

Analysis, Analyzation

Analysis is the preferred and less pompous word to use.

Analyst, Annalist

Analyst is someone skilled at studying or analyzing problems.
The systems analyst spends much time at the computer.

Annalist is someone who writes historical records.
The annalist recounted the events that shaped World War II.

Anchors away, Anchors aweigh

Anchors aweigh is the correct phrase. The word *weigh* originates from an old word meaning heave, hoist, or raise. *Aweigh* means something, in this case an anchor, has been raised.
The captain called anchors aweigh as the ship prepared to leave.

Androgenous, Androgynous

Androgenous refers to producing male offspring.
The chromosome prompts the formation of androgenous embryoids.

Androgynous refers to having both male and female characteristics.
The androgynous offspring surprised the researchers.

Note: Sometimes the word **hermaphrodite** is used as a synonym for **androgynous**.

Anecdote, Antidote

Anecdote is a short account (usually funny) about an incident.
Alex told us many amusing anecdotes about his time in college.

Antidote is a medicine or remedy for fighting poison or disease.
The doctor prescribes antidotes to counteract any poison.

Annals, Annual, Perennial

Annals is a compiled record of events; an **annual** is a plant that grows for just one year (or season); and a **perennial** is a plant that grows for many years.

Annihilate, Decimate

Annihilate means to destroy something completely.
*The company uses a spray to **annihilate** the lawn weeds.*

Decimate literally means to destroy one tenth of something, but is commonly used to mean destroying a large part of something.
*The strong weed killer could **decimate** many parts of the lawn.*

Annunciate, Enunciate

Annunciate, a rare word, means to announce or proclaim.
*In the event of trouble, the system **annunciates** an alarm.*

Enunciate means to pronounce, articulate, or set forth precisely.
*The statements **enunciate** their position on conservation issues.*

Antagonist, Protagonist

Antagonist refers to an adversary or opponent.
*Once close friends, they became **antagonists** later in life.*

Protagonist is a leading character in a play, novel, or story.
*The **protagonist** in tonight's play also serves as the narrator.*

Protagonist, meaning a proponent, is becoming more common.
*Tony is a **protagonist** of solar energy and reduced emissions.*

Ante, Anti

Ante means before or in front of something.
*The abbreviation A.M. stands for **ante** meridian (before noon).*

Anti means against or opposed to something.
*To combat the poison effectively, the doctor needs an **anti**toxin.*

Antecedence, Antecedents

Antecedence is the act of going before in time.
*Please make the reservation with at least one month of **antecedence**.*

Antecedents are people or things that have gone before.
*Her **antecedents** left her a fortune, and she invested all of it.*

Antenna, Antennae, Antennas

Antenna is the metallic apparatus for sending or receiving electromagnetic waves. **Antennae** is the plural form of *antenna* or the sensory appendage on an insect's head. **Antennas** can also be the plural form of *antenna*.

Antibody, Antigen

Antibody is protein produced by the body that fights bacteria and other foreign substances. **Antigen** is any substance that causes your immune system to produce antibodies.

Anticipate, Expect

Anticipate means to foresee and prepare for something.
*The college **anticipates** a large enrollment jump next year.*

Expect means to look forward to a likely occurrence.
*The college **expects** most of the senior class to get job offers.*

Anticlimatic, Anticlimactic

Anticlimactic is the correct word.

Antisocial, Asocial, Unsocial, Unsociable

Antisocial means angry, hostile, or harmful to society. **Asocial** means rejecting or lacking the capacity for social interaction (a recluse). **Unsocial** (the preferred word) or **unsociable** means the same as **asocial**.

Anxious, Eager

Anxious means nervous, worried, or filled with anxiety.
*Harry is **anxious** about his final grades in math and science.*

Eager means looking forward to or earnestly longing.
*Greg is **eager** to see how well he did in math and science.*

Any body, Anybody

Any body refers to any single person or thing.
*Did he talk with **any body** in the office about the problem?*

Anybody refers to any person.
***Anybody** can talk to the administration about the problem.*

Any more, Anymore

Any more means some more.
*Annie and Mary do not want **any more** problems with their cars.*

Anymore means now.
*Our friends do not live here **anymore**, and we miss them.*

Any one, Anyone

Any one refers to any single person or thing.
*Did you listen to **any one** of the new holiday CD releases?*

Anyone refers to any person.
*Did **anyone** in the class see the solar eclipse yesterday?*

Any thing, Anything

Any thing refers to one of many things.
*You can choose **any thing** in the store to purchase.*

Anything refers to any occurrence, object, or matter.
***Anything** related to music will be discussed at the workshop.*

Any time, Anytime

Any time means one of many times.
***Any time** the team scores, the fans are delighted.*

Anytime means at any time.
*They can attend the meeting **anytime** they wish.*

Any way, Anyway

Any way means by a choice of methods.
*Joe tries to improve his car's performance **any way** he can.*

Anyway means in any case or nevertheless.
***Anyway**, George is attending the concert despite his late start.*

Anyways, Anywheres

Always use **anyway** and **anywhere**.

Apparent, Evident

Apparent should be used when there is a matter of doubt.
*It is **apparent** that Tim could win the school election.*

Evident implies the existence of external signs of some sort.
*His disappointment was not **evident**.*

Apple Cider, Apple Juice, Apple Vinegar

Apple Cider is *unpasteurized* apple juice that becomes *cider*
once it ages. **Apple Juice** is *pasteurized* juice from pressed
apples. **Apple Vinegar** is fully aged and fermented *apple cider*.

Apportion, Portion, Proportion

Apportion means to distribute or divide.
*The attorney wants to **apportion** the shares of stock evenly.*

Portion, as a noun, means a limited amount of something.
*The family wants to leave a big **portion** of the estate to charity.*

Portion, as a verb, is a synonym for *apportion* (distribute or divide).
*The family wants to **portion** part of the large estate to charity.*

Proportion means a ratio of one thing to another.
*The **proportion** of golfers to tennis players increases every year.*

Appose, Oppose

Appose means to place near one another or to juxtapose.
*The box's edges should be **apposed** and slightly turned in.*

Oppose means to act adversely or in opposition.
*The senator says he would **oppose** the bill if put to a vote.*

Apposite, Opposite

Apposite means appropriate, pertinent, or suitable.
*Her style of acting and singing is **apposite** for the lead part.*

Opposite means altogether different or to the contrary.
*The producer has an **opposite** view about casting the lead.*

Appraise, Apprise

Appraise means to estimate, evaluate, or judge something.
*Have someone **appraise** your ring; then properly insure it.*

Apprise means to advise or inform.
*Please **apprise** the accused person of his constitutional rights.*

Appropriate, Apropos

Appropriate means suitable or fitting.
*The timing of John's promotion could not be more **appropriate**.*

Apropos means in regard to, incidentally, or relevant.
***Apropos** next week's meeting, now we cannot attend.*
***Apropos**, where is the schedule you promised us a week ago?*

Apt, Likely

Apt refers to a habitual tendency.
*Religious people are **apt** to pray and attend services regularly.*

Likely refers to a high probability.
*It's **likely** we will see our grandchildren over the holidays.*

Arbiter, Arbitrator

These words are synonyms.

Arc, Ark

Arc refers to something shaped with a curved or bowed line.
*In geometry, a segment of a curve is called an **arc**.*

Ark refers to a large, flat-bottomed boat.
*In the Old Testament, Noah built an **ark** for survival.*

Arcane, Archaic

Arcane means mysterious or clearly understood by just a few.
*Today their **arcane** ideas are the framework of our processes.*

Archaic means antiquated or no longer applicable.
*Once the **archaic** methods are over, we will see better results.*

Arctic, Artic

Always use **arctic**, not **artic**, as in **Arctic** Circle.

Area, Aria

Area refers to a region or section.
*To help us place you, what **area** of engineering is your specialty?*

Aria refers to a solo vocal piece.
*When the tenor finished his **aria**, they graciously applauded.*

Argument, Quarrel

An **argument** refers to a discussion or debate usually not involving anger.
*An **argument** between attorneys is not uncommon in courts.*

A **quarrel** is a dispute or disagreement usually involving anger.
*The umpire and the manager had a **quarrel** during the game.*

Armory, Arsenal

An **armory** is a storehouse for weapons, and an **arsenal** is a supply of weapons.

Aroma, Odor

Aroma refers to a pleasing smell (*cake's aroma*), and **odor** (*a kitchen's foul odor*) refers to an unpleasant smell.

Around, About

Around should refer to a physical proximity or surrounding.
*We'll look for you **around** the front of the building.*

About indicates an approximation.
*Let's get to the course and tee off after work **about** 5.*

Arraignment, Indictment

Arraignment is formally calling a defendant to answer a charge.
*The judge postponed the **arraignment** for a week.*

Indictment is formally charging a defendant with a crime.
*The grand jury handed up an **indictment** against five people.*

Arrant, Errant

Arrant means confirmed, downright, or extreme.
*Many of us found the story nothing short of **arrant** nonsense.*

Errant means wandering or roving.
*Ray's **errant** tee shot on the last hole cost him the tournament.*

Arrhythmic, Eurhythmic

Arrhythmic refers to lacking rhythm or the regularity of rhythm.
*During the hospitalization phase, slight **arrhythmic** disorders registered in 10 patients.*

Eurhythmic refers to the art of graceful and harmonious movement (dancing).
*The class includes basic **eurhythmic** and choreography techniques.*

Artery, Vein

An **artery** carries blood from the heart to other parts of the body while a **vein** carries blood to the heart.

Artful, Arty

Artful means skillful or clever.
*He's been **artful** about bypassing the planning regulations.*

Arty means artistic.
*In addition to van Gogh, the **arty** group has many heroes.*

Arthroscopic, Orthoscopic

Arthroscopic is the correct word.
*His injured right knee required immediate **arthroscopic** surgery.*

Articulate, Eloquent

Articulate refers to enunciating clearly and effectively.
*Bill is a most **articulate** speaker with a wealth of experience.*

Eloquent refers to expressing oneself persuasively, vividly, or movingly.
*She is an **eloquent** speaker, and we could listen to her for hours.*

Artisan, Artist, Artiste

Artisan refers to one skilled in a trade.
*Ed is an accomplished **artisan** whose passion is wood furniture.*

Artist refers to anyone engaged in the fine or performing arts.
*Marcel Marceau, a pantomime **artist**, was born in 1923.*

Artiste refers to an entertainer or anyone skilled in a special craft.
*The chef at Lake Mohonk is considered a real **artiste**.*

As, Like

As is a conjunction and is followed by a subject and verb.
*In the cold winter, he hibernates **as** a bear does.*

Like is a preposition and should be followed by an object.
*In the cold winter, he hibernates **like** a bear.*

As if, As though

Either phrase is acceptable, but grammarians prefer **as though**.
*You describe the film's details **as though** you have seen it.*

As time passed, As time progressed

Use **as time passed** because time does not *progress*.
***As time passed**, the animal became more domesticated.*

Ascent, Assent

Ascent means an upward climb or any movement upward.
*The mountain's slight **ascent** requires little climbing experience.*

Assent means to agree or concur with something.
*The teacher **assented** to accepting Jessica's late paper.*

Ascribe, Subscribe

Ascribe means to attribute to a source or author.
*Though this statement is usually **ascribed** to our president, it was actually written by a reporter.*

Subscribe means to agree with or to give assent.
*Many people do not **subscribe** to these conspiracy theories.*

Assail, Assault, Battery

Assail or **assault** is the threat of physical harm, and **battery** is the actual physical harm to another person.

Assay, Essay

Assay, a verb, means to evaluate or analyze something.
*Take time to **assay** the information before drawing a conclusion.*

Essay, as a verb, means to make an attempt.
*The baby boy **essayed** a few wobbly steps last week.*

Essay, a noun, is a short composition expressing an author's opinion.
*Pat has to write an **essay** on Tolstoy for her literature class.*

Assert, Claim

Assert means to state or express firmly.
*The party's leader **asserts** she could not support the proposal.*

Claim means to demand or ask for as one's own.
*It is his birthday, so Larry is **claiming** the first piece of cake.*

Assonance, Consonance

Both words are sound devices typically used in poetry and song that serve as building blocks to verse. **Assonance** is the repetition of similar vowel sounds of words close together ("Hear the m**e**llow w**e**dding b**e**lls."—*Edgar Allan Poe*). **Consonance** is the repetition of middle or ending consonant sounds of words close together ("And the **s**ilken **s**ad un**c**ertain ru**s**tling of each purple curtain."—*Edgar Allan Poe*).

Assume, Presume

Assume means to take for granted without evidence.
*Though it is common, do not **assume** fluoride is in your water.*

Presume means to take for granted, usually because evidence exists.
*The van is being serviced, so we **presume** it is not running well.*

Assure, Ensure, Insure

Assure means to make confident or promise something.
*I **assure** you payment is in the mail and delivery is imminent.*

Ensure means to make certain something will happen.
*Mailing the package by Friday **ensures** a Tuesday delivery.*

Insure means to buy insurance.
*Because of its value and size, we **insured** the package.*

Asteroid, Meteor, Meteorite, Meteoroid

An **asteroid** is a celestial body of rock and metal that moves around the sun. A **meteor** is a bright trail in the sky when a *meteoroid* is heated to incandescence by friction with the earth's atmosphere (also called *falling star*, *meteor burst*, or *shooting star*). A **meteorite** is a *meteoroid* that reaches earth as a metal or rock. A **meteoroid** is a moving celestial object that is smaller than an *asteroid*.

Astrology, Astronomy

Astrology is the study of the positions and aspects of celestial bodies presuming they can influence earthly occurrences and human affairs. **Astronomy** is the study of celestial bodies and the universe as a whole.

Astronaut, Cosmonaut

An **astronaut** is an American who travels in space, and a **cosmonaut** is a Russian who travels in space.

At least, Leastways

Leastways is awkward. Use **at least**.
*That's not much of an achievement, **at least** (not **leastways**) not for him.*

Atlas, Gazetteer

An **atlas** is a bound map collection, and a **gazetteer** is a geographical dictionary or index usually found at the back of an *atlas*.

Atmosphere, Stratosphere
The **atmosphere** is the gaseous layer surrounding earth, and the **stratosphere** is the layer of **atmosphere** between 7 and 50 miles up.

Attaché, Briefcase
An **attaché** is a slim carrying case for carrying mainly paperwork. A **briefcase** is a larger carrying case that comes in varying sizes and shapes and carries more than just paperwork.

Attain, Obtain
Attain means to accomplish something.
*We wish Scott well in striving to **attain** his educational goals.*

Obtain means to get possession of something.
*Scott is determined to **obtain** his doctorate by next year.*

Attenuate, Extenuate
Attenuate means to weaken, diminish, or lessen.
*The judge **attenuated** his sentence due to questionable evidence.*

Extenuate means to excuse by minimizing the seriousness.
*Saying sorry did not **extenuate** the crime.*

Attorney, Lawyer
In everyday usage and American English, the terms are synonyms; however, per some dictionaries, a **lawyer** can provide legal advice and has been trained all about laws. An **attorney** is *legally permitted* to represent people or act in their behalf.

Note: Some attorneys and lawyers use just the word *Esquire* before their names.

Audubon, Autobahn
Audubon usually refers to John James Audubon, the famous painter of birds, or to the bird conservation society founded in his name.
*Connie purchased a painting that was a genuine **Audubon**.*

Autobahn is the famed system of highways in Germany with no speed limits.
*Connie cruised the **Autobahn** at over 100 kilometers per hour.*

Auger, Augur

Auger refers to a tool for drilling holes.
*To drill holes for deck supports, Andy uses an electric **auger**.*

Augur means to predict or to be a sign of something.
*Recent developments could **augur** change for the car industry.*

Augment, Supplement

Augment means to increase in size, degree, or effect.
*Some people **augment** their income with Internet businesses.*

Supplement, as a verb, means to add something or make up for a deficiency.
*The doctor told Laura to **supplement** her diet with vitamins.*

Supplement, as a noun, means something added.
*The new part-time job was a **supplement** to her full-time job.*

Aural, Oral

Aural refers to the ear or to the sense of hearing.
*The young class has more success learning by **aural** methods.*

Oral refers to things of the mouth.
*The hygienist always does an **oral** exam before the cleaning.*

Authentication, Authentification

The correct spelling is **authentication**.
*We signed a certificate of **authentication** for the buyer.*

Authoritarian, Authoritative

Authoritarian means requiring absolute obedience to authority.
*Does **authoritarian** government always involve censorship?*

Authoritative means approved by a proper authority.
*The nutritionist is writing an **authoritative** guide to eating well.*

Autocracy, Autonomy

Autocracy refers to a dictatorship.
*The Poles struggled against Nicholas II and the Russian **autocracy**.*

Autonomy refers to self government.
*The local government should have full fiscal **autonomy**.*

Avalanche, Landslide

An **avalanche** refers to snow, rocks, or other debris coming down a mountainside. A **landslide** is an entire mountainside coming down.

Avenge, Revenge

Avenge means to seek a fair settlement for a wrong.
*The hockey team hopes to **avenge** last year's loss to Albany.*

Revenge means to retaliate for a wrong.
*The tenant damaged things as **revenge** for the eviction notice.*

Avert, Avoid, Divert

Avert means to prevent or ward off something.
*Moderate exercise and diet can sometimes help **avert** weight gain.*

Avoid is to shun or stay clear of something.
*Tom tries to **avoid** the tough questions at a press conference.*

Divert is to turn aside, distract, or turn from one course to another.
*I can **divert** an incoming call to a cell phone with that feature.*

Avocation, Evocation, Vocation

Avocation refers to something one does outside of work.
*As we imagined, Celeste's true **avocation** is gardening.*

Evocation means spiritually summoning something through the power of the mind.
*"The **evocation** of that better spirit."*—M. Arnold

Vocation refers to a profession, principal endeavor, or livelihood.
*Their **vocation** is responding to other people's needs.*

Avow, Vouch

Avow means admitting or declaring something publicly.
*I **avow** that the education at Potsdam State is excellent.*

Vouch means supporting the claims of something or someone.
*I can **vouch** for her dedication, honesty, and sincerity.*

Award, Reward

Award refers to something given as a prize.
*John received an **award** for his antique tractor display.*

Reward refers to something given for a good deed or service.
*The firefighter received a **reward** for saving the child's life.*

Axel, Axle

Axel refers to a difficult jump in figure skating (named after Norwegian figure skater Axel Paulsen). **Axle** refers to a shaft on which a wheel or set of wheels revolves.

Axiom, Axion

Axiom is an established truth, rule of law, or principle.
*This **axiom** treats crime as a wrong done to another person not breaking the law.*

Axion is a hypothetical particle of matter with no charge or spin and small mass.
*One can identify this energy density as a bunch of **axion** particles found in galaxies.*

B

"The ill and unfitting choice of words wonderfully obstructs the understanding."—Francis Bacon

Backward, Backwards

Backward is preferred in American usage.

Bad, Badly

Bad is an adjective describing nouns or pronouns.
*Our family has a **bad** feeling about the whole thing.*
*John felt **bad** about missing Karen's surprise party.*

Badly is an adverb.
*Despite few rehearsals, the band is not playing **badly**.*

Baited, Bated

Baited means to entice or lure something.
*We **baited** the mousetrap with peanut butter.*

Bated means to lessen the force or intensity of something.
*The team waited with **bated** breath to see who won the game.*

Baleful, Baneful

Baleful refers to something that menaces or foreshadows evil.
*The teacher's **baleful** look helped silence the noisy students.*

Baneful refers to something harmful or destructive.
*The virus is having **baneful** effects on the farmer's cattle.*

Balmy, Barmy

Balmy means pleasant or soothing.
*Spain's **balmy** climate allows for a long golf season.*

Barmy means mad.
*You would have to be **barmy** to visit England without trying its pastries.*

Baloney, Bologna

Baloney is nonsense; **bologna** is sausage or lunch meat.

Baluster, Banister

A **baluster** is a short pillar that supports a handrail.
*The **balusters** on the deck were secured with small screws.*

A **banister** is the handrail on a staircase.
*We slid down the **banister** when we were children.*

Barb Wire, Barbed Wire, Bob Wire

Though variations exist, the correct phrase is **barbed wire**.
*They replaced the **barbed wire** with a new barrier type.*

Barbarism, Barbarity

Barbarism is a crude or rude act or an incorrect expression of words.
*Reputable magazines would never tolerate such **barbarisms**.*

Barbarity refers to savage brutality or cruelty in actions.
*Accounts of the dictator's **barbarity** shocked many countries.*

Barely than, Barely when

Barely when is the correct expression.
***Barely** had we left the area **when** our car suddenly died.*

Basal, Basil

Basal refers to a foundation that forms a base while **basil** refers
to an herb.

Basement, Cellar

A **basement** is the substructure or foundation of a building. A
cellar is an underground shelter or space.

Bathos, Pathos

Bathos is insincere or overdone sentimentality.
*The play was just so much **bathos** that it became annoying.*

Pathos is that element in literature that stimulates pity or sorrow.
*The film captured all the **pathos** of their situation.*

Batter, Dough

Batter is a thin mixture of flour and liquid (usually poured).
*Brian is whipping up some **batter** for more blueberry pancakes.*

Dough is a thick mixture of flour, liquid, and other things.
*To raise money for her class, she sold frozen cookie **dough**.*

Battery, Assail, Assault

*See entry for **Assail, Assault, Battery**.*

Bazaar, Bizarre

Bazaar refers to a market where miscellaneous goods are sold.
*Nancy and Joan traveled to a local **bazaar** to scout antiques.*

Bizarre means strange, weird, or out of the ordinary.
*His **bizarre** behavior disrupts the entire class.*

Be sure and, Be sure to

Be sure to is the correct phrase.
*Please **be sure to** leave an e-mail address and phone number.*

*Jane found a pair of **bizarre** boots at the church **bazaar**.*

Beaut, Butte

Beaut is an abbreviation for *beauty*, and **butte** refers to a hill or mountain with a steep slope.

Because of, Due to

Because of refers to cause and effect.
Because of the band canceling, ticket holders are quite upset.

Due to should be used with a linking verb (*is*, *are*, *was*, etc.).
*The band's cancellation is **due to** poor ticket sales.*

Beckon call, Beck and call

Beck and call is the correct phrase. The word *beck* is a shortened form of *beckon*, which means to make a mute signal or gesture to call someone over.
*Unlike major newspapers, they don't have a research team at their **beck and call**.*

Behest, Request

Behest refers to an authoritative command or urging.
*At his **behest**, we made an appointment to see the dentist today.*

Request means to ask for something.
*The dentist **requests** that we try to avoid hard candy.*

Being as, Being that

Avoid these phrases in writing. Use **because** instead.
***Because** my car broke down, I missed my starting time.*

Believe, Feel, Think

Believe refers to a conviction or principle.
*He **believes** regular jogging is good for the heart.*

Feel refers to a sense or perception.
*We still **feel** the effects of the aftershock.*

Think refers to an opinion.
*She **thinks** her interview went exceptionally well.*

Bell, Belle

Bell is an instrument that rings when struck, and **belle** refers to an attractive or popular woman.
*The southern **belle** rang the **bell** before entering the house.*

Bemuse, Amuse

*See entry for **Amuse, Bemuse**.*

Benefactor, Beneficiary

Benefactor refers to someone who provides a gift.
*The university recognizes that Jim is a long-time **benefactor**.*

Beneficiary refers to someone who receives something.
*Tanya was the **beneficiary** of several research grants.*

Benevolence, Malevolence

Benevolence means being inclined to do charitable acts.
*His **benevolence** to the homeless was well known.*

Malevolence means wishing harm to others.
*The **malevolence** of a few destroyed his political aspirations.*

Benign, Malignant

Benign means not dangerous, and **malignant** means life threatening.

Berth, Birth

Berth refers to a ship's dock space, a sleeping space, or a place for a vehicle to park. **Birth** refers to being born.

Beside, Besides

Beside as a preposition means next to or compared to.
*The commissioner sat **beside** him at the awards dinner.*

Besides as a preposition means in addition to or otherwise.
***Besides** winning the math award, Jane is on the honor roll.*
*Who **besides** me likes his latest book?*

Besides as an adverb means moreover.
***Besides**, Al needs more than expensive clubs to lower his score.*

Between, Among
*See entry for **Among, Between**.*

Between you and I, Between you and me
Always use **between you and me**.

All prepositions, such as *between*, take pronouns in the **objective** case (*it, her, him, me, them, us, you*) not in the nominative case (*he, I, it, she, they, we, you*) or possessive case (*her, hers, his, its, mine, my, our, ours, their, theirs, your, yours*).
*Just **between you and me,** we are having a party for the family.*

Biannual, Biennial
Biannual, a synonym for *semiannual*, means twice a year.
*Donna and John make **biannual** visits to North Carolina.*

Biennial means once every two years.
*The car registration is due for its **biennial** renewal.*

Bigamy, Monogamy, Polygamy
Bigamy means being married to just two spouses at the same time; **monogamy** means being married to only one person; **polygamy** means having multiple spouses at the same time.

Bilateral, Multilateral, Unilateral
Bilateral, meaning two-sided, refers to two agreeing entities.
*The city has a **bilateral** agreement with the sports arena.*

Multilateral, meaning many-sided, refers to more than two agreeing entities.
*The company has a **multilateral** agreement with all four firms.*

Unilateral, meaning one-sided, refers to an entity acting alone.
*We have a **unilateral** agreement on free trade with that country.*

Billiards table, Pool table
Unlike a **pool table**, a **billiards table** has no pockets.

Bimonthly, Semimonthly
Bimonthly means occurring every two months.
*We bought the refreshments for the **bimonthly** status meeting.*

Semimonthly means occurring twice a month.
*Our **semimonthly** reports are due the first and third Friday of each month.*

Note: The same rules apply to *biweekly, biyearly, semiweekly,* and *semiyearly.*

Bisect, Dissect

Bisect means to divide into two equal or identical parts.
*The diagonals of a parallelogram **bisect** each other.*

Dissect means to cut apart and examine something.
*The students plan to **dissect** the preserved frog next week.*

Bite, Byte

Bite is a snack, and **byte** is 8 binary digits processed by a computer.

Blackout, Brownout

Blackout is a total electrical power failure over a large area.
*In 1965 and 1989, **blackouts** affected areas of New York.*

Brownout is an interruption or temporary drop of electrical power.
*A **brownout** caused my computer screen to flicker a few times.*

Blatant, Flagrant

Blatant is an adjective meaning obvious.
*We made a **blatant** mistake by overlooking Gary's contributions.*

Flagrant means notoriously evil, bad, or objectionable.
*The crew of the ship had an open and **flagrant** mutiny.*

Blithe, Blither

Blithe means happy and carefree.
*Zack's **blithe** attitude to his work gives it a certain freshness.*

Blither refers to talking and babbling foolishly.
*Amid the **blither** of the debate, it was fine political theatre.*

Bloc, Block

Bloc is a coalition of people, groups, or nations with a common goal.
*Italy, France, and Spain formed a **bloc** to promote trade.*

Use **block** for all other meanings.

Blond, Blonde

Blond refers to a boy or a man. **Blonde** refers to a girl or a woman.

Boar, Boor, Bore

Boar refers to a male pig.
*After the 4-H fair, Amy washed her prize-winning **boar**.*

Boor refers to a crude, unrefined, or insensitive person.
*He sometimes can be a loud, obnoxious **boor** during meetings.*

Bore refers to being dull, tiresome, or tedious.
*Reading was a **bore** until he discovered Harry Potter books.*

Boarder, Border

Boarder is a person that rents a room at a house (sometimes with meals included), and **border** is a boundary between areas or the outer edge of something.

Bode, Bowed

Bode refers to predicting or foretelling, and **bowed** refers to things shaped like a **bow**.

Bolder, Boulder

Bolder refers to being more daring or courageous, and **boulder** refers to a large rock.

Bona fide, Bonafied

Bona fide is the correct spelling.
*I wouldn't consider his radio show a **bona fide** news program.*

Boom to the economy, Boon to the economy

Boon to the economy, meaning a timely economic benefit or state, is the correct phrase.

*The new factory will be a **boon to the economy**.*

Born, Borne

Born means brought into life. It also is used to indicate one has a natural talent for something.

*His first son was **born** on Father's Day.*
*Bruce is so fast, people say he was **born** to run.*

Borne means to be carried or to endure something.

*Lyme disease is the most common tick-**borne** disease.*
*He has **borne** their mistakes with the patience of a saint.*

Bough, Bow

Bough refers to a branch on a tree, and **bow** refers to the front part of a ship.

Bought, Boughten

Bought is the past tense of *buy*. **Boughten** is not a word.

Bouillon, Bullion

Bouillon refers to clear, seasoned soup usually made from beef.

*The **bouillon** has no MSG and only 1 gram of fat per serving.*

Bullion refers to gold or silver.

*Brokers of **bullion** act as agents for buyers and sellers.*

Bourgeois, Proletariat

Bourgeois refers to the middle class. **Proletariat** refers to the lower class.

Bow, Port, Starboard, Stern

With regard to a ship, the **bow** is the front, **port** is the left side, **starboard** is the right side, and **stern** is the back.

Boycott, Embargo

Boycott is the refrain of business or social relations to show protest.
*The consumers are **boycotting** all the company's products.*

Embargo is a government prohibition on trade with another nation.
*In 1987, England imposed a trade **embargo** on Iran.*

Braise, Braze

Braise means to cook slowly under a covered container.
*The chef **braises** his vegetables in lemon juice and butter.*

Braze means to solder something.
*The plumber needs to **braze** all the pipe fittings in the house.*

Bran new, Brand new

Brand new, an expression meaning new (think of a *brand* coming fresh out of the fire) is the correct phrase. It has nothing to do with a product's name.
*They looked forward to moving into the **brand new** house.*

Breach, Breech

Breach is an infraction or violation of some kind.
*By leaving the job site, Bob is guilty of a **breach** of contract.*

Use **breech** for all other meanings, such as **breech** delivery.

Breadth, Breath, Breathe

Breadth refers to distance, width, or scope.
*Damian's success reflects the **breadth** of his experience.*

Breath is the noun and **breathe** is the verb.
*We typically take several **breaths** when we **breathe** heavily.*

Bridal, Bridle

Bridal refers to a marriage ceremony.
*The **bridal** party stayed at the reception until 2 a.m.*

Bridle refers to the harness on a horse or to horseback riding.
*Make sure the horse's **bridle** is not too tight but yet snug.*
*Though the **bridle** path is long and winding, it is still enjoyable.*

Bridle also refers to restraint or control.
*The players should **bridle** their appetites before exercising.*

Briefcase, Attaché

A **briefcase** is a larger carrying case that comes in varying sizes and shapes and carries more than just paperwork. An **attaché** is a slim carrying case that carries mainly paperwork.

Bring, Take

Bring means to carry something toward some place.
*When you finish writing the plan, please **bring** it to my office.*

Take means to carry something away from some place.
*When I finish reviewing the plan, please **take** it to your office.*

British Isles, Great Britain, United Kingdom

The **British Isles** consists of the **United Kingdom** and its islands (Orkneys, Shetlands, and the Isle of Man). **Great Britain** consists of England, Scotland, and Wales. The **United Kingdom** consists of Great Britain and Northern Ireland.

Broach, Brooch

Broach means to open, introduce, or bring up something.
*Do not **broach** that subject with the other team members.*

Brooch refers to a pin or ornament with a clasp.
*Donna wore an expensive **brooch** to her high school reunion.*

Brochure, Leaflet, Pamphlet

A **brochure** is a small booklet usually not longer than 24 pages.
A **leaflet** is a small printed item usually not longer than 4 pages.
A **pamphlet** is a stapled publication with fewer than 100 pages.

Broken, Busted

Prefer **broken**. **Busted** is considered a nonstandard word.
*Scott suffered a **broken** leg during Monday's football practice.*

Brother-in-laws, Brothers-in-law

Brothers-in-law is the correct phrase.

Build off of, Build on

Build on is the correct phrase.
Build on the successes you have attained this year.

Burglary, Robbery, Theft

Burglary means breaking into a building to steal something.
Burglaries plagued the new development.

Robbery is the taking of one's property by threat or force.
London's Great Train Robbery of 1963 involved 20 people.

Theft is the taking of one's property without threat or force.
Identity theft is a fast growing crime in America.

(Note: *Larceny* is the legal term for theft or stealing.)

Buttocks, Buttox

Buttocks is the correct spelling.

By and large, By in large

By and large, meaning generally or as a rule, is the correct phrase.
By and large they recruit engineers more than any other position.

*The **burglar** was **robbed** as he ran from the bank.*

C

"An unusual word should be shunned as a ship would shun a reef."
—Julius Caesar

Cache, Cachet, Cash

Cache is a hiding place.
*The bears found a **cache** of food belonging to some hunters.*

Cache also is small, fast computer memory that holds recently accessed data.
*Could the **cache** handle the extra memory requirements?*

Cachet refers to a mark of authenticity, prestige, or quality.
*The state courts have a **cachet** that the local courts lack.*

Cash is ready money.
*His wallet was fat with **cash** when he left the poker game.*

Caesar, Ceasar

Both the Roman emperor and the salad dressing are spelled identically (**Caesar**).

Calamity, Calumny

Calamity is a great misfortune or disaster.
*A hurricane would be a **calamity** for this low coastal region.*

Calumny is a falsehood maliciously made to hurt one's reputation.
*The charges were pure **calumny** in an effort to embarrass them.*

Calendar, Calender, Colander

Calendar is the correct spelling for a system of recording time.
Calender is an old word that refers to a machine used in finishing paper and cloth. A **colander** is a perforated, bowl-shaped kitchen utensil for draining liquids and rinsing food.

Callous, Callus

Callous refers to having an unfeeling attitude.
Perhaps you're being too callous about their situation.

Callus refers to a thickening or hardening of the skin.
The tight running shoes gave Austin a callus on his foot.

Calvary, Cavalry

Calvary, with a capital *C,* is the place in Jerusalem where Christ died. **Cavalry** are soldiers mounted on horseback.

Can, Could, May, Might

Can and **could** refer to capability, though **could** often implies some doubt.
Unlike our previous server, this one can support up to 50 users.
I suppose our old car could make the drive to California.

May and **might** refer to permission or possibility.
When time permits, you may start working on the project.
If everything goes as planned, you may finish the project early.
We might be able to go to the party after the game.

Can not, Cannot

Though no difference in meaning exists between these two words, **cannot** as one word is the more acceptable spelling.

Cancel, Delay, Postpone

Cancel means to stop something with no intent to reschedule.
After three years, Eric decided to cancel his subscription.

Delay means to put off until further notice.
The heavy rains could delay the game for several hours.

Postpone means to cancel with the intent to reschedule.
I hope the committee does not postpone the test another week.

Cannon, Canon

Cannon refers to a large gun or a shot in billiards.
*Every Labor Day, soldiers shoot the **cannons** at West Point.*
*In some billiards, they allow four points for a **cannon**.*

Canon refers to a law or ruling laid down by the church.
*The Book of **Canons** is a collection of 151 **canon** laws of the Church of England.*

Canter, Cantor

Canter refers to a horse's gait.
*The thoroughbred's **canter** is one of strength, agility, and grace.*

Cantor refers to a singer, usually in a house of worship.
*Expect Lori as one of the **cantors** for this weekend's service.*

Canvas, Canvass

Canvas is the cloth used in tents or sails, or what painters use.
*You can enlarge photos on **canvas** to look like paintings.*

Canvass is getting political support from voters.
*As usual, Rob opted to **canvass** in his own neighborhood first.*

Capacity, Ability

*See entry for **Ability, Capacity**.*

Capital, Capitol

Capital refers to money, property, uppercase letters, a form of punishment, architecture, or the location of a government seat.
Examples:
The **capital** gain tax, **capital** letters, **capital** punishment, the pillar's **capital,** or the **capital** of New York State is Albany.

Capitol refers to buildings in which state or national government meet. (The *C* in **Capitol** is usually uppercase.)
Examples:
The **Capitol** in downtown Albany or **Capitol** Hill.

Capitulate, Recapitulate

Capitulate means to surrender, come to terms, or acquiesce.
*NATO forced the country to **capitulate** to its demands.*

Recapitulate means to sum up, review briefly, or repeat.
*Let us **recapitulate** what we have learned these last two days.*

CAPITOL

Welcome to Springfield Capital of Illinois

*The **Capitol** building is in the **capital** city.*

Carat, Caret, Carrot, Karat

Carat is a measurement (200 milligrams) used in weighing gemstones.
*Ty bought an engagement ring that had a 1.5-**carat** diamond.*

Caret is a proofreader's mark (^) to indicate insertion. It's also used in math to indicate exponentiation.
*Editors often insert many **carets** on a writer's first draft.*
*If the **caret** is not in the formula, you will get a different answer.*

Carrot is the orange root that Bugs Bunny enjoys eating.
***Carrots** grow best when planted in spring.*

Karat is a measurement showing the ratio of pure gold to other materials in an alloy. The measurement uses a base of 24 units. Pure gold, which is 24/24ths gold, is called 24-karat gold.
*All their 12-**karat** jewelry is on sale through next weekend.*

Card shark, Cardsharp

A **card shark** is a proficient, cutthroat, honest card player, and a **cardsharp** is a swindler.

Cardinal numbers, Ordinal numbers

Cardinal numbers (*1*, *five*, *247*, *etc.*) show quantity, not order.
*Despite all the traffic, we arrived **one** hour early for the concert.*

Ordinal numbers (*first*, *second*, *third*, *etc.*) show order or numerical sequence.
*Unlike in other years, this year our seats are in the **third** row.*

Careen, Career, Carom

Careen means to swerve or tilt while in motion.
*Despite improved suspension, the car **careened** during the race.*

Career means to move at full speed.
*The stock cars **careered** down the track.*

Carom means to collide and rebound.
*We held our breath as a few racing cars **caromed** off the wall.*

Carnivorous, Herbivorous, Omnivorous

Carnivorous refers to eating meat (or flesh).
*These **carnivorous** dinosaurs are from the Cretaceous period.*

Herbivorous refers to eating only plants.
*The iguanas and tortoises are typical **herbivorous** reptiles.*

Omnivorous refers to eating everything.
*An **omnivorous** diet consists of meats, fruits, grains, and vegetables.*

Case and point, Case in point

Case in point, meaning an example that supports a point, is the correct phrase.
*The low-carb diet works. I'm a **case in point**.*

Cease the day, Seize the day

Seize the day, which means to make the most of every moment, is the correct phrase.
*"**Seize the day**, put no trust in the morrow."*—Horace

Cellar, Basement

A **cellar** is an underground shelter or space. A **basement** is the substructure or foundation of a building.

Cement, Concrete

Cement is a powdery binding material that consists of clay and limestone. **Concrete** is a mixture of sand, gravel, and other materials all held together by **cement**.
*The workers are installing a **concrete** (not **cement**) sidewalk.*

Censer, Censor, Censure, Sensor

Censer is a container used for burning incense.
*The church acquired a new gold-plated **censer**.*

Censor, as a verb, means to suppress objectionable material.
*Do they have a legal right to **censor** material on the Internet?*

Censor, as a noun, is the person examining certain material.
*Are the TV **censors** approving the subject matter for broadcast?*

Censure means to blame, criticize strongly, or condemn.
The principal censured the teacher for failing to comply.

Sensor is a device that receives and responds to a signal or stimulus.
Most cars produced after 1980 have an oxygen sensor.

Centenarian, Centurion

A **centenarian** is a person who lives to be 100, and a **centurion** is a Roman army commander.

Center around

An impossibility. Use *center about*, *center in*, or *center on*.
Today's Open House centers on the theme of Quality at Work.

Century, Millennium

A **century** is 100 years, and a **millennium** is 1,000 years.

Ceremonial, Ceremonious

Ceremonial means being proper for a ceremony.
She wore her traditional ceremonial dress to the banquet.

Ceremonious means done in great ceremony (politely or formally).
The new king offered a ceremonious toast at the gala.

Cession, Session

Cession refers to an act of ceding (surrendering).
It took the committee over two years to ratify the cession agreement.

Session refers to a meeting or term.
Scott is taking one course during the school's summer session.

Chafe, Chaff

Chafe means to irritate or annoy something.
The new running shoes chafed John's feet.

Chaff, as a verb, means to tease good-naturedly.
Patty's teammates chaffed her for being late again to practice.

Chaff, as a noun, are husks separated from seeds during threshing.
The field workers literally separated the wheat from the chaff.

Chaise longue, Chaise lounge

Chaise longue is the correct phrase. The phrase is French for *long chair* with a back support and seat long enough to support outstretched legs.

Chalked full, Chock full

Chock full, meaning completely full, is the correct phrase. Of navel origin, the saying comes from the phrase *chock-a-block*, which refers to two blocks of tackle stuck together so tightly they can't be tightened any further.
*The technician recommended a web site **chock full** of useful tools.*

Champ at the bit, Chomp at the bit

Champ at the bit is the correct phrase. The expression, which means eager or impatient, refers to an excited horse biting (*champing*) its bit. Because of constant misuse, *chomp at the bit* is becoming more common.
*James **champs at the bit** when he sees the other soccer team take the field.*

Chantey, Shanty

Chantey refers to a song sung by sailors while working.
*As the crew washed the deck, the captain requested a **chantey**.*

Shanty refers to a roughly built shack.
*While stranded on the island, the crew lived in a small **shanty**.*

Character, Reputation

Character refers to a person's personality.
*His spontaneous reaction is completely out of **character**.*

Reputation refers to the external perception of a person.
*In spite of her **reputation** as fair, she was not a good umpire.*

Cheap, Inexpensive

Cheap describes something that has a low price and is of low quality.
*We filled our first apartment with **cheap**, second-hand furniture.*

Inexpensive means low cost.
*The software was **inexpensive**, but did the job perfectly.*

Child-care, Child care

Hyphenate this phrase when used as an adjective.
*They've used a **child-care** agency for many years.*

Do not hyphenate this phrase when used as a noun.
*They searched everywhere for the best **child care**.*

Childish, Childlike

Childish means inappropriately acting like or resembling a child.
*The painting looks like **childish** scribble rather than creative art.*

Childlike means retaining some positive attributes of childhood.
*Even in his 60s, Ken retains a **childlike** love of rock music.*

Chord, Cord

Chord refers to a group of musical notes.
*Many of the group's earlier hits consisted of just three **chords**.*

Cord refers to a vocal cord, a cord of wood, or a rope.
*The high notes and fast tempo strained his vocal **cords**.*
*To be on the safe side, I bought two **cords** of wood for winter.*
*Please pull the **cord** when you get to the back door.*

Choreography, Chorography

Choreography refers to the art of dance design, and **chorography**
refers to the art of map making.

Chow, Ciao

Chow is slang for food, and **ciao** is the Italian word for hello or
goodbye.

Chronic, Acute

*See entry for **Acute, Chronic**.*

Cite, Sight, Site

Cite means to quote or mention something.
*When you write a term paper for Dr. Hards, **cite** your references.*

Sight is something seen, an ability to see, the foreseeable future, or an optical instrument.
*The ship's passengers soon caught **sight** of the beautiful island.*
*The passengers **sighted** the island from a mile out.*
*Unfortunately, there is no compromise or solution in **sight**.*
*Before target practice, John adjusts the **sight** on his rifle.*

Site refers to a location.
*The natural terrain lends itself to being a good **site** for a house.*

Citizen, Resident

A **citizen** is someone who has the full rights of a nation, either by birth or naturalization. A **resident** lives in a community but doesn't necessarily have the rights of a citizen.

Claim, Assert

*See entry for **Assert, Claim**.*

Clamber, Clamor

Clamber means to climb with difficulty and effort.
*While trying to **clamber** the wall, he caught his shoe and fell.*

Clamor means to shout, to make noise, to protest, or to demand.
*The questions from the crowd eventually rose to a loud **clamor**.*
*Many people joined the public **clamor** to keep the school open.*

Classic, Classical

Classic refers to a long-established, usually high, standard.
*Babe Ruth had a **classic** baseball swing.*

Classical refers to the arts, literature, and architecture of ancient Greece and Rome. In music, **classical** means music from the 18th century European tradition, as opposed to pop or rock.
*Molly would rather play **classical** piano pieces.*

Cliché, Clique

Cliché is an overused expression.
*Good writers usually try to avoid using **clichés** in their writing.*

Clique refers to a small, exclusive group of people.
*To the dismay of some, many **cliques** exist in their high school.*

Click, Press, Type

Click means pressing and releasing the mouse button once.
*To start the program, **click** the red icon on the desktop.*

Press means to put force on something.
*If it fails again, **press** the Reset button on the computer once.*

Type means pressing a character key on a keyboard.
*After you have entered all the data, **type** the word EXIT.*

Climactic, Climatic

Climactic refers to the culmination of events (a climax).
*The special effects in the **climactic** scene of the film are dull.*

Climatic refers to meteorological conditions.
*The Ice Age ushered in severe **climatic** conditions.*

Climax, Acme

*See entry for **Acme, Climax**.*

Cohere, Adhere

*See entry for **Adhere, Cohere**.*

Collaborate, Corroborate

Collaborate means to aid, cooperate, or work together.
*The church **collaborated** on the holiday project for the needy.*

Corroborate means to strengthen by confirming something.
*The witness **corroborated** the defendant's testimony.*

Collectable, Collectible

Either spelling is acceptable.

College, University

A **college** mainly grants bachelor's degrees. A **university** grants bachelor's, master's, and doctorate degrees.

Collision, Collusion

Collision refers to a crash.
*The sudden **collision** of the two ships raises serious questions.*

Collusion refers to a secret agreement between parties.
*The high prices in winter could be the result of **collusion** among the companies.*

Cologne, Perfume

Cologne is a weak, relatively inexpensive fragrance. **Perfume** is a strong, relatively expensive fragrance.

Comedian, Comedienne

Comedian refers to a male comic, and **comedienne** refers to a female comic.

Common, Mutual, Ordinary, Popular

Common means widespread or prevalent.
*That type of mosquito is a **common** disease carrier.*

Mutual means shared by two or more parties.
***Mutual** trust is a key ingredient for a long-term relationship.*

Ordinary means plain or undistinguished.
*Her high grades reflect studying habits that are far from **ordinary**.*

Popular means especially liked or preferred by the masses.
*Children everywhere play the **popular** game.*

Compare and Contrast

A redundancy. When you **compare** things, you note both differences and similarities. When you **contrast** things, you note just the differences. Therefore, use **compare** or **contrast** separately but not together.

Compared to, Compared with

Compared to and **compare with** often are used interchangeably, but **compare to** can mean liken, while **compare with** always means differences are being examined.

*The author and entertainer **compared** his world **to** a stage.*
***Compared with** 1996, the 2000 election was problematic.*

Compendium, Compilation

A **compendium** is a **compilation** of information.

Complacent, Complaisant

Complacent refers to a feeling of self-satisfaction, to the point that one becomes lazy.
*After much success, the film director grew **complacent**.*

Complaisant refers to a willingness to comply or oblige.
*An energetic and **complaisant** guide gave us a tour of campus.*

Complement, Compliment

Complement, as a noun, is a group that completes a set.
*A **complement** of four people would now bring the staff to nine.*

Complement, as a verb, means to go well with something.
*The four new people would **complement** the rest of the staff.*

Compliment, as a noun, is an expression of courtesy or praise.
*The supervisor gave the staff a **compliment** on its work.*

Compliment, as a verb, means to praise or respect something.
*The supervisor regularly **compliments** the staff on its work.*

Compose, Comprise

Compose means to create or to make up the whole.
*John Williams **composes** musical scores for Spielberg films.*
*Five thousand songs **compose** the college's new music library.*

Comprise means to consist of something.
*The college's new music library **comprises** 5,000 songs.*

Memory hook: The whole **comprises** the parts, and the parts **compose** the whole.

Comprehensible, Comprehensive

Comprehensible means understandable or intelligible.
*Despite all the technical jargon, the book is **comprehensible**.*

Comprehensive means comprising many things or large in scope.
*Jim did a **comprehensive** study on Internet sales.*

Comptroller, Controller

Comptroller is a variant spelling for **controller**. Both words refer to the chief accountant in an organization. **Comptroller** is usually used in government-related positions, and **controller** is more common in private industry.

Compulsion, Compunction

Compulsion refers to a forced impulse, compliance, or drive.
*Lennon had a **compulsion** to make the Beatles a top rock band.*

Compunction refers to remorse or regret for one's actions.
*He showed much **compunction** about leaving his old job.*

Compulsive, Compulsory, Impulsive

Compulsive refers to feeling compelled about something.
*Tom **compulsively** cleans his car.*

Compulsory refers to being obligated to do something.
*Les took a **compulsory** physical examination for his new job.*

Impulsive refers to doing things on the spur of the moment.
*Occasionally Ed gets **impulsive** and buys expensive wine.*

Concave, Convex

Concave means curved inward like the inside of a circle, and **convex** means curved outward like the outer boundary of a circle.

Concede, Accede, Exceed

*See entry for **Accede, Concede, Exceed**.*

Concert, Recital

Concert refers to a performance given by two or more people.
The Beatles last American concert was in 1966.

Recital refers to a performance given by one person (a soloist).
Her Christmas piano recital went better than anyone expected.

Concurrent, Consecutive

Concurrent means simultaneous or happening at the same time.
Management held concurrent meetings at all company sites.

Consecutive means successive or following one after the other.
The pitcher threw six consecutive strikes during the last inning.

Conducive to, Conducive with

Conducive to is the preferred phrase.
Good working conditions can be conducive to productivity.

Confectionary, Confectionery

Confectionary is the place where you buy confections, and
confectionery is a sweet such as candy or ice cream.

Confidant, Confidante, Confident

Confidant refers to a male trustworthy friend; **confidante** the
female trustworthy friend.
Dennis is his confidant as well as his legal advisor.

Confident refers to being self assured.
Liam is confident that his unique house design will be sold.

Congenial, Congenital, Genial

Congenial means having the same nature, disposition, or tastes.
We work in a congenial atmosphere that all of us enjoy.

Congenital means existing in an individual since birth.
His health problems can be traced to a rare congenital disorder.

Genial means agreeable, pleasing, or compatible.
The retirees are traveling and enjoying Hawaii's genial climate.

Connote

Connote, Denote

Connote means to imply or suggest something.
*His actions **connote** he is unhappy living there.*

Denote means to indicate or refer to specifically.
*We were just taught the symbol for pi **denotes** the number 3.14159.*

Note: **Connote** and **denote** are preferable to *connotate* and *denotate*, which are considered obsolete.

Conscience, Conscious

Conscience means a sense of right and wrong.
*His **conscience** didn't bother him when he fired his friend.*

Conscious means to be aware of something or to be awake.
*I made a **conscious** decision to practice my tuba lessons daily.*
*Though he hit his head, he was **conscious** after the accident.*

Consequent, Subsequent

Consequent means following as a direct result.
*Her great evaluation and **consequent** pay raise made her day.*

Subsequent means occurring after.
***Subsequent** to the installation, my desktop icons do not load.*

Consistently, Constantly

Consistently means steadfast, unwavering, or without change.
*Airline tickets **consistently** rank among the most popular Internet items.*

Constantly means unceasing, perpetual, or without interruption.
*In a **constantly** changing technical world, training is essential.*

Consonance, Assonance

Both words are sound devices typically used in poetry and song that serve as building blocks to verse. **Assonance** is the repetition of similar vowel sounds of words close together ("Hear the mellow wedding bells."—*Edgar Allan Poe*). **Consonance** is the repetition of middle or ending consonant sounds of words close together ("And the silken sad uncertain rustling of each purple curtain."—*Edgar Allan Poe*).

Consul, Council, Counsel

Consul is an official representing one's country in another country.
*A new **consul** was appointed last week for the Republic of Chad.*

Council is a group appointed or elected to make decisions.
*Most cities and towns have a **council** that governs certain areas.*

Counsel, as a noun, is an attorney; as a verb, it means to give advice.
*His **counsel** (attorney) did an excellent job of building a case.*
*The social worker tried unsuccessfully to **counsel** the parents.*

*The **counsel** told the **consul** what to say to the city **council**.*

Contagious, Infectious

Contagious refers to diseases spread through physical contact.
If you deal with contagious diseases, disinfect your hands well.

Infectious refers to diseases spread through air, water, etc.
We are exposed to chemicals and infectious diseases.

Note: In figurative use, these words can be synonymous.
Her optimistic and humorous mood is infectious (or contagious).

Contemptible, Contemptuous

Contemptible means worthy of contempt or deserving scorn.
The board thinks Keith's treatment of the intern is contemptible.

Contemptuous means expressing a feeling of contempt.
They risk disciplinary action for making contemptuous remarks.

Content, Context

Content refers to what's inside and **context** refers to a setting.
My quote in the paper was taken out of context (not content).

Contentious, Controversial

Contentious means argumentative or quarrelsome.
The measure was defeated after a contentious House debate.

Controversial refers to subjects being arguable or debatable.
They extended the deadline on the controversial change.

Conterminous, Contiguous

Conterminous means contained within one boundary.
The conterminous United States excludes two states: Alaska and Hawaii.

Contiguous means sharing a boundary or touching.
The suburb of Oak Park is contiguous with Chicago.

Continual, Continuous

Continual means repeatedly, but not necessarily without interruptions.
Jane continually ignores her boss' requests for more coffee.

Continuous means constantly or without interruptions.
*The border runs **continuously** from the river to the mountains.*

Continuance, Continuation

Continuance refers to the duration of a state or condition.
*Her **continuance** in office depends on the November election.*

Continuation refers to the resumption of something.
*Today's meeting is just a **continuation** of yesterday's meeting.*

Contrary, Converse

To be **contrary** means to differ or disagree with something.
Contrary to belief, Joe was a good football coach.

Converse means the opposite of something.
*We held the **converse** view that the executive was effective.*

Convert into, Convert to

Convert into means to change from one thing to another.
*The tool **converts** PDF documents **into** HTML or ASCII text.*

Convert to means to switch allegiance, loyalty, or obligation.
*While attending college, John **converted to** another faith.*

Convince, Persuade

Convince means causing someone to believe through evidence.
*His minty breath **convinced** the teacher that Fred had brushed his teeth.*

Persuade means causing someone to act through reasoning.
*The class **persuaded** Diane to run for re-election in the spring.*

Copyright, Copywrite

Copyright is the correct word. Though **copywrite** is not a word, copywriters do exist. Those people write copy for things like ads, brochures, sales letters, etc.

Core, Corps

Core refers to a central or essential part.
*A **core** rule of their company is a strict dress code.*

Corps refers to people acting as a body rather than individuals.
*He and a few other people we know belong to the Peace **Corps**.*

Corespondent, Correspondent

Corespondent is a person charged with adultery in a divorce suit.
*The **corespondent** never admitted to an affair with the woman.*

Correspondent is a communicator, such as a writer.
*Kathy worked as a special **correspondent** for the network.*

Cornet, Coronet

A **cornet** is the musical instrument. A **coronet** is a small crown, headband, or the upper margin of a horse's hoof.

Corrode, Erode

Corrode means to be eaten away by a chemical reaction.
*The rust will immediately **corrode** the brass if it is not removed.*

Erode means to wear away by water or wind.
*The heavy spring rains **eroded** the high cliffs by their house.*

Note: Both of these words can also be used figuratively.
*Mistrust can **corrode** any good business partnership.*
*Confidence in their leadership **eroded** over the years.*

Cosmonaut, Astronaut

A **cosmonaut** is a Russian who travels in space, and an **astronaut** is an American who travels in space.

Could care less, Could not care less

Though it is a cliché, **could not care less** is the correct phrase.
*He **could not care less** about learning how to play bridge.*

Could have, Could of

Could have is the correct phrase.
*During last night's meeting, you **could have** heard a pin drop.*

Councilor, Counselor

A **councilor** serves on a council, and a **counselor** offers counsel and advice.

Country, Nation

A **country** is a piece of land or area and the home of certain people. A **nation** is a body of people associated with a particular area or territory.

Coup de grâce, Coup de gras

Coup de grâce, meaning a decisive event, is the correct phrase.
If they are defeated today, it could be their **coup de grâce**.

Couple, Few

Couple refers to only two, and **few** refers to anything above two.
Our presentation received only a **couple** *of questions by a* **few** *people.*

Covert, Overt

Covert means concealed, covered, or hidden.
Mike's company provides **covert** *video surveillance equipment.*

Overt means open to view, plain, apparent, or public.
England continues to offer the United States its **overt** *support.*

Cramp my style, Crimp my style

Cramp my style is the correct phrase.

Cream de mint, Crème de menthe

Crème de menthe is the correct phrase.

Credible, Creditable, Credulous

Credible means believable.
Though it's a strange and unusual story, it seems **credible**.

Creditable means worthy of praise or credit.
The band gave a **creditable** *performance in Syracuse.*

Credulous means gullible.
Even a **credulous** *fan doesn't believe seats are still available.*

Crevasse, Crevice

Crevasse is a deep opening or crack usually found in a glacier.
*Fran is standing too close to the **crevasse** of the glacier.*

Crevice is a narrow opening or crack in a wall, floor, or rock.
*A bat can find the smallest **crevice** to sleep in during the day.*

Crises, Crisis

Crises is the plural form and takes a plural verb.
*Banking **crises** can have devastating effects on many economies.*

Crisis is the singular form and take a singular verb.
*Addressing the banking **crisis** is a necessary step for recovery.*

Criteria, Criterion

Criteria is the plural form; **criterion** is the singular form.
*They identified 10 important **criteria** for their business plan.*
*The most important **criterion** for us is customer acceptance.*

Note: Phrases such as *a criteria, one criteria,* or *this criteria*
should be avoided. Also, a few writing authorities accept
criterions as the plural of **criterion**.

Critique, Criticize

Critique (noun or verb) means a critical review of something.
*The professor's film **critique** annoyed some people.*
*Professor Ward **critiques** movies for the* Saratoga Press.

Criticize means to offer critical remarks about something.
*Tim **criticized** Walter for his indifference to politics.*

Croquet, Croquette

Croquet is a lawn game using mallets, balls, and wickets.
*Historians say **croquet** began as an outdoor version of billiards.*

Croquette is a small cake of minced food usually coated in bread
crumbs and deep fried.
*Beef stock, spices, potatoes, and meat made up the **croquette's**
filling.*

Cue, Queue

Cue refers to a signal to begin something.
*The actors are getting their **cues** from the orchestra conductor.*

Queue refers to people or things in line.
*Is that your document or someone else's in the print **queue**?*

Currant, Current

Currant is a small red or black berry and part of the raisin family.
Currants are grown for their use in jams, jellies, and preserves.

Current is a flow of water or air in a direction, a flow of electricity, or the present time.
*Changes in water density can affect some ocean **currents**.*
*An electric **current** is usually thought of as a flow of electrons.*
*The **current** system of state control lacks accountability.*

Curtains, Draperies

Curtains are smaller, less fancy, and typically easier to hang than **draperies**.

Cut and dried, Cut and dry

Cut and dried, which means finished, is the correct expression. The phrase comes from the timber industry, and refers to an area that has been cut clear of trees (clear cut).
*The supervisor's plans are not as **cut and dried** as you think.*

Cynical, Sarcastic, Skeptical

Cynical means contemptuously distrustful of someone's motives.
*"Those **cynical** men who say that democracy cannot be honest and efficient."*—FDR

Sarcastic means using bitter or caustic language against someone.
*The **sarcastic** clerk cost the store many customers.*

Skeptical means doubting, questioning, or mistrustful.
*Candy seemed **skeptical** when I told her I am seeing a psychic.*

Cynosure, Sinecure

Cynosure refers to something that strongly attracts attention.
*"Where perhaps some beauty lies, the **cynosure** of neighboring eyes."*—Milton

Sinecure refers to a position or office that requires little or no responsibilities.
*"A lucrative **sinecure** in the Excise."*—Macaulay

D

"A word in earnest is as good as a speech."—Charles Dickens

Damage, Damages
Damage refers to destruction of some kind.
*The sun's UVA and UVB rays can permanently **damage** the skin.*

Damages refer to compensation awarded by a court of law.
*The court awarded substantial **damages** to the affected families.*

Damp, Dank
Damp refers to moisture, humidity, or slightly wet.
*The air was too **damp** to dry anything on the clothes line.*

Dank means disagreeably damp, humid, or moist.
*The humid conditions made their finished basement quite **dank**.*

Dare say, Daresay
Either spelling is acceptable.

Data, Datum
Data is the plural of **datum**.
*The Census Bureau collects these **data** from each agency.*

Note: In technical writing, **data** (as a collective noun) often takes a singular verb.
*The online numeric **data** is restricted to privileged users.*

Daughter-in-laws, Daughters-in-law
Daughters-in-law is the correct phrase.

Daylight saving time, Daylight savings time
Daylight saving time is the correct phrase.

Dazed, Dazzled

Dazed means shocked or stunned.
*After the surgery, he appeared **dazed** and unsure of where he was.*

Dazzled means blinded by intense light or amazed by a spectacular display.
*The brilliant setting sun **dazzled** our eyes.*
*The figure skater **dazzled** the audience with her jumps.*

Deadly, Deathly

Deadly means likely to cause death.
*Research shows aspirin can reduce the risk of **deadly** infections.*

Deathly means like or in the manner of death.
*After the loss, a deathly **silence** fell across the stadium.*

Dearth, Plethora

Dearth refers to a great shortage or scarcity of something.
*We have a **dearth** of competent workers to handle the project.*

Plethora refers to an abundance or excess of something.
*The holiday season brings a **plethora** of "Greatest Hits" CDs.*

Debar, Disbar

Debar means to bar from a place or to prevent from exercising a right.
*Many states **debar** people under 21 from alcohol and tobacco.*

Disbar means to expel from the bar or the legal profession.
*He avoided prosecution, but they may still **disbar** him.*

Debark, Disembark

Both words mean to go ashore or to unload something. Either is acceptable.

Decadence, Decadents

Decadence means showing low morals and a love for world pleasures. It can also mean being artificial or lacking in quality.
*The acceptable level of moral **decadence** has plunged recently.*
*Unfortunately, he exhibited **decadence** in his dress and manner.*

Decadents are spoiled people with low morals and a love for worldly pleasures.
*Some of their wealthiest members can be labeled as **decadents**.*

Decent, Descent, Dissent

Decent means proper or honest.
*The play's interpretation was done in a **decent** manner.*
*Many people consider Rick a thoughtful and **decent** individual.*

Descent means a downward slope or family origin.
*The airplane's sudden **descent** alarmed many passengers.*
*When one mentions the **descent** of man, we think of Darwin.*

Dissent means disagreement.
*If the cause made real sense, there would not be much **dissent**.*

Decided, Decisive, Incisive

Decided means clear-cut, unmistakable, or without doubt.
*This company has a **decided** advantage over its competitors.*

Decisive means conclusive.
*The committee's **decisive** action gave our firm an advantage.*

Incisive means acute, cutting, or sharp.
*The company lost an **incisive** mind and an outstanding engineer.*

Decimate, Annihilate

*See entry for **Annihilate, Decimate**.*

Decry, Descry

Decry means to openly condemn or ridicule something.
*The faculty has a right to **decry** the cuts in the budget.*

Descry means to see or catch sight of, often from a distance.
*Some nights you can actually **descry** the blue whales out at sea.*

Deduce, Deduct, Adduce

*See entry for **Adduce, Deduce, Deduct**.*

Deductive, Inductive

Concerning types of reasoning:

Deductive means to reason from the general to the specific (top-down approach).
Example: *All people need water to survive; Bob is a person; Bob needs water to survive.*

Inductive means to reason from the specific to the general (bottom-up approach).
Example: *Bob needs water to survive; Bob is a person; all people need water to survive.*

De facto, De jure

De facto means actual.
The de facto speed limit on a busy afternoon is only 50 m.p.h.

De jure means as a matter of law or right.
The maximum speed limit, de jure, is 65 m.p.h.

Defective, Deficient

Defective means faulty.
The scanner's defective circuit board can easily be replaced.

Deficient means lacking completeness or a key ingredient.
Tests proved her diet was deficient in calcium and magnesium.

Deference, Difference, Diffidence

Deference means courteous regard or respect.
The young reporter showed deference to the famous anchor.

Difference means a distinguishing characteristic or disparity.
The difference is in how they present themselves to the public.

Diffidence means reserved, shy, or lacking self confidence.
Overcoming their diffidence may lead to better opportunities.

Definite, Definitive

Definite means certain, precise, explicit, or clear.
After the game, I had a definite feeling of accomplishment.

Definitive means final, decisive, and authoritative.
The interested party immediately gave us a definitive answer.

Defuse, Diffuse

Defuse means to remove a fuse (usually from an explosive).
*The company hired an explosives expert to **defuse** the bomb.*

Diffuse means to spread out.
*The mouse's odor **diffused** throughout the entire house.*

Degenerate, Deteriorate

Degenerate is a decline in quality or virtue.
*His latest CD shows a **degenerate** pattern of poor production.*

Deteriorate is a weakening or the wearing away of something.
*The building has weakened and is beginning to **deteriorate**.*

Delay, Cancel, Postpone

*See entry for **Cancel, Delay, Postpone**.*

Delegate, Relegate

Delegate means to assign others to a task.
*The officials may **delegate** authority to the appropriate people.*

Relegate means send or consign to an obscure place or position.
*After I fell, I was **relegated** to a backup spot on the team.*

Deluge, Flood

A **deluge** is a large, heavy downpour of water that typically does not leave damage. A **flood** is overflowing water that covers land. It typically leaves damage.

Delusion, Allusion, Illusion

*See entry for **Allusion, Delusion, Illusion**.*

Demur, Demure

Demur means to voice opposition, objection, or delay.
*Jim may **demur** at the suggestion that we start the meeting now.*

Demure means modest, reserved, or shy.
*Peter appears **demure** despite all of his accomplishments.*

Denote, Connote

*See entry for **Connote, Denote**.*

Denounce, Renounce

Denounce means to criticize or condemn something openly.
*The new drug was **denounced** as ineffective and harmful.*

Renounce means to give up claim to something.
*The engineer willingly **renounced** all ownership to the software.*

Dependant, Dependent

In American English, **dependent** is used as both a noun and an adjective. British English has a distinction between the words.

Depose, Dispose

Depose means to remove someone from a position (or power) or to take one's testimony.
*Employees want to **depose** him from his high company position.*
*Investigators will **depose** the witness behind close doors.*

Dispose means to settle affairs or be inclined to do something.
*The lawyer appointed Celeste to **dispose** our mother's estate.*
*Please **dispose** of your trash before leaving the theater.*

Depraved, Deprived

Depraved means morally bad or corrupt.
*A **depraved** person can have a bad influence on other people.*

Deprived means lacking economic or social necessities.
*We distributed the food baskets to **deprived** neighborhoods.*

Deprecate, Depreciate

Deprecate means to disapprove of or belittle something.
*Tom **deprecated** his contributions to the company's success.*

Depreciate means to lower the value or worth of something.
*Years of city driving drastically **depreciated** my car's value.*

Descension, Dissension

Descension means to descend, fall, or sink.
*The team's sudden **descension** in the rankings surprised many.*

Dissension means disagreement or a difference of opinion.
Dissension exists over where the new town hall should be built.

Desert, Dessert

Desert, as a noun, is an arid place with little vegetation or something deserved or merited, especially a punishment.
*The Southwest **desert** ranges are beautiful places to visit.*
*When the plan was revealed, they received their just **deserts**.*

Desert, as a verb, means to abandon or forsake.
*Despite financial setbacks, he refuses to **desert** the company.*

Dessert, the noun, is the sweet thing one eats at the end of a meal.
*After dinner, we usually stop at the bakery for **dessert**.*

Desolate, Dissolute

Desolate means uninhabited or miserable.
*Chris and Bill decided to retire in a **desolate** part of Maine.*
*The children are **desolate** over the loss of their dog last year.*

Dissolute means lacking in moral standards.
*I regret having lived a **dissolute** lifestyle in my younger years.*

Despatch, Dispatch

Dispatch is preferred in American usage.

Desperate, Disparate

Desperate means nearly hopeless or undertaken as a last resort.
*We are taking **desperate** measures to avoid another strike.*

Disparate means completely distinct or different.
*The candidates' ideas reflect **disparate** visions of government's role.*

Despise, Hate

Despise means to regard with contempt or to look down on.
*It's their successful economy that is so **despised** by the group.*

Hate means to dislike intensely or loathe something.
*It seems people either love or **hate** mayonnaise on sandwiches.*

Detract, Distract

Detract means to take away a part or to lessen something.
*Their odd behavior **detracts** from their accomplishments.*

Distract means to divert, confound, or harass something.
*The noise in the balcony **distracted** her attention from the play.*

Device, Devise

Device refers to a gadget.
*In addition to the PC, the personal copier is a useful **device**.*

Devise means to think of something.
*The President and his staff **devised** a plan to help the economy.*

Dexterous, Dextrous

Though **dexterous** is more common, either spelling is correct.

Diagnosis, Prognosis

Diagnosis is the identification of a problem, most commonly a medical condition.
*The **diagnosis** is a slight tear in the right knee's cartilage.*

Prognosis is a forecast or prediction.
*The doctor offered his **prognosis** that knee surgery would help.*

Dialate, Dilate

Dilate is the correct word.

Dialect, Accent

*See entry for **Accent, Dialect**.*

Dialectal, Dialectical

Dialectal refers to a dialect or a regional language.
*Nine major **dialectal** regions exist in China.*

Dialectical refers to a method for arriving at the truth.
*Some philosophers use the Socratic **dialectical** method of cross-examination.*

Dialog, Dialogue

Though **dialogue** is more common, either spelling is acceptable.

Differ from, Differ with

Differ from means to differ between one person or thing and another.
*My car **differs from** Joe's in that it is equipped with a GPS.*

Differ with means to differ in opinion (disagree).
*I **differed with** her opinion of the new school principal.*

Different from, Different than

Different from is used when comparing items.
*Excluding cost, her car is **different from** mine in many ways.*

Different than is used when a subject and verb (a clause) follow the phrase.
*Her job today is much **different than** it was five years ago.*

Dilemma, Problem, Quandary

Dilemma is a situation that requires a choice between undesirable options.
*The chairperson is caught in a **dilemma** between lying and admitting he embezzled the money.*

Problem is a situation, matter, or person that presents perplexity or difficulty.
*They have a **problem** with the supervisor's leadership.*

Quandary is a situation that requires a choice between more than two things.
*We're in a **quandary** about which one of the three films would we enjoy most.*

Diminish, Minimize

Diminish means to reduce, shrink, or make less important.
*Glycolic acid can help **diminish** facial lines and wrinkles.*

Minimize means to reduce to the smallest degree or size.
*Exercises to the stomach muscles can **minimize** back pain.*

Diplomat, Diplomate

Diplomat is one skilled in negotiations, good manners, and tact.
The diplomat offered an effective resolution to the conflict.

Diplomate is a physician certified as a specialist by a medical board.
Dr. Walker is a diplomate of the American Board of Plastic Surgery.

Disapprove, Disprove

Disapprove means to withhold approval of something.
Do you disapprove of the way Lou is handling his job?

Disprove means to prove the falsity of something.
Even if you disprove Jim's claim, he may file again.

Disassemble, Dissemble

Disassemble means to take something apart.
To disassemble the hardware, follow the instructions.

Dissemble means to disguise or conceal behind a false appearance.
The man attempted to dissemble his guilt with laughter.

Disassociate, Dissociate

Either spelling is acceptable, though **dissociate** is preferred.
He tried to dissociate himself from their questionable activities.

Disburse, Disperse

Disburse means to pay out or expend.
Accounting should disburse the travel compensation next week.

Disperse means to scatter something.
The road crew will disperse the road salt before rush hour.

Disc, Disk

Disc refers to optical media (audio CDs, DVDs, cushions in one's spine). **Disk** refers to magnetic media (floppy disk, hard drives).

Discomfit, Discomfort

Discomfit means to frustrate, disconcert, or baffle.
Their questionable comments may discomfit the employees.

Discomfort means pain, uneasiness, or distress.
*Helen's sprained wrist gave her **discomfort** during the match.*

Discover, Invent

Discover means to find something already in existence, but unknown.
*While on the expedition, Pete **discovered** a few new species.*

Invent means to create something new.
*Edison **invented** many useful devices for society.*

*The men **dispersed** as soon as the pay was **disbursed**.*

Discovered Missing

This is a contradiction. Just say **missing**.

Discreet, Discrete

Discreet means to be careful about what one does or says.
*If you ask for a raise, be **discreet**; I don't want Jim to know.*

Discrete means separate or distinct.
*The conversion process consists of five **discrete** steps.*

Discrepancy, Disparity

Discrepancy is a difference between facts or claims.
*The appraised value and the asking price show a **discrepancy**.*

Disparity means inequality or incongruity.
*We found a big **disparity** between their ideals and their actions.*

Discriminate, Distinguish

Discriminate means to perceive differences and use that perception to make a judgment.
*The players could not **discriminate** between a good golf hole and a bad one.*

Distinguish means to recognize qualities or features of a thing that make it different from others.
*The groundskeeper could easily **distinguish** bent grass and Kentucky blue grass.*

Disenfranchise, Disfranchise

Disfranchise is preferred in American usage.

Disinformation, Misinformation

Disinformation refers to deliberately misleading information.
*The competition gave us **disinformation** about their products.*

Misinformation refers to incorrect information.
*The paper printed **misinformation** about the concert dates.*

Disingenuous, Ingenious, Ingenuous

Disingenuous means devious, dishonest, or pretending.
*He's being rather **disingenuous**, saying the computer runs well.*

Ingenious means clever, imaginative, or original.
*Art developed an **ingenious** solution to the hardware problem.*

Ingenuous means candid, honest, or innocent.
*Jill and Rick have an open, **ingenuous** manner that people like.*

Disinterested, Uninterested

Disinterested means impartial, neutral, objective, or unbiased.
*We chose Maria as a **disinterested** third party to decide our fate.*

Uninterested means bored, indifferent, or simply not interested.
*Despite Tom's elaborate proposal, his boss remains **uninterested** in the project.*

Disorganized, Unorganized

Disorganized means thrown into disorder or disarray.
*We have never seen a dormitory room so **disorganized**.*

Unorganized means not yet organized or lacking order.
*Though the league started last year, it still appears **unorganized**.*

Disorientated, Disoriented

Disoriented, meaning to feel displaced, is the preferred spelling.
*Lori felt groggy and **disoriented** after her long flight.*

Disparage, Disparate

Disparage means to criticize or belittle someone.
*His comment was not meant to **disparage** a nice guy like Ed.*

Disparate means different or distinct in quality or kind.
*The local charity event brought many **disparate** people together.*

Dispense with, Dispose of

Dispense with means to do without something.
*We would like to **dispense with** all the unnecessary paperwork.*

Dispose of means to get rid of something.
*Where can I properly **dispose of** the used oil and paint thinner?*

Displace, Misplace

Displace means to shift, change, or move.
*Last summer the raging floods **displaced** many residents.*

Misplace means to lose something or put it in the wrong place.
*It's easy to **misplace** a punctuation mark in a complex sentence.*

Dissatisfied, Unsatisfied

Dissatisfied means not satisfied and has a critical connotation.
*They were **dissatisfied** with the food and service at the diner.*

Unsatisfied also means not satisfied, but doesn't necessarily imply criticism.
*His hunger was **unsatisfied** despite the large meal he ate.*

Dissect, Bisect

*See entry for **Bisect, Dissect**.*

Distinct, Distinctive

Distinct means clearly apparent, discrete, separate, or obvious.
*A **distinct** improvement in giving helped many families last year.*

Distinctive means distinguished or standing out as different.
*J. Hayward's **distinctive** voice has won the band many fans.*

Distraught, Diswraught

Distraught is the correct word.

Disused, Unused

Disused means no longer in use.
*Developers recently bought the **disused** airfield.*

Unused means not used.
***Unused** flight coupons must be returned with the claim form.*

Diversity, Adversity

*See entry for **Adversity, Diversity**.*

Divert, Avert, Avoid
*See entry for **Avert, Avoid, Divert**.*

Doctor, Physician
Doctor refers to anyone who has been granted a doctor's degree. **Physician** is a general term for a doctor of medicine, someone legally qualified to practice medicine. All physicians are doctors of medicine, but not all doctors practice medicine.

Doggy dog world, Dog-eat-dog world
Dog-eat-dog-world is the correct phrase. It means that the world is ruthlessly competitive and derives from a sixteenth century proverb that people may revert to the animal laws of survival.
*With shrinking markets, it's now a **dog-eat-dog world** for many companies.*

Dogmatic, Pragmatic
Dogmatic means arrogantly authoritative or overbearing.
*His **dogmatic** and demanding personality did not fit in well here.*

Pragmatic means practical.
*Pat takes a **pragmatic** approach to teaching children.*

Dominant, Dominate, Domineer
Dominant means commanding or controlling over all others.
*The largest wolf is usually **dominant** in the pack.*

Dominate means to control, govern, or regulate something.
*Their software **dominates** the financial services industry.*

Domineer means to exercise arbitrary or overbearing control.
*The strong will of a few can sometimes **domineer** a community.*

Dosage, Dose
Dosage refers to a regimen of something and **dose** refers to a specific amount.
*Patients received an initial **dose** of 20 mg and thereafter a **dosage** of 10 mg twice a day for a month.*

Doubtful, Dubious

Doubtful means to be uncertain.
*It's **doubtful** if we will ever know who technically won the election.*

Dubious refers to doubt or uncertainty about something.
*The official gave a **dubious** reply when asked about the proposed tax cut.*

Dough, Batter

*See entry for **Batter, Dough**.*

Douse, Dowse

Douse means to extinguish or wet thoroughly.
*The firefighters **doused** the flames with water most of the night.*

Dowse means to look for water or minerals with a divining rod.
*It was common for the pioneers to **dowse** for water on the trail.*

Down the pike, Down the pipe

Down the pike is the correct phrase. It means something is going to happen. The Pike was originally a huge entertainment area at the 1904 St. Louis World's Fair. Fair goers would commonly say, *There's always something new coming down the Pike.*

Downfall, Drawback

Downfall refers to the destruction of something.
*The Russian Revolution led to Czar Nicholas II's **downfall**.*

Drawback refers to a flaw or problem of some kind.
*Their plan to camp there had one **drawback**: too many gnats.*

Downward, Downwards

Downward is preferred in American usage.

Draperies, Curtains

Curtains are smaller, less fancy, and typically easier to hang than **draperies**.

Drowned, Drownded

Drowned is the correct word.

Dual, Duel

Dual refers to something in a pair.
*After you install the **dual** carburetors, open the throttle half way.*

Duel is a formal battle or contest intended to settle a dispute.
*"**Duel** of the Titans" is a film about Romulus and Remus.*

Duck tape, Duct tape

Duct tape is the correct phrase.
*We told them to use **duct tape** to seal the doors and windows.*

Due to, Because of

*See entry for **Because of, Due to**.*

Dwarf, Midget

A **dwarf** is a very short person with disproportionate body parts, and a **midget** is a very short person with proportioned body parts. Because these two words have fallen out of favor, prefer the terms *short person* or *little person*.

E

"Every word was once a poem."—Ralph Waldo Emerson

E-Business, E-Commerce
E-Business refers to conducting general business on the Internet.
E-Commerce refers specifically to the buying and selling of goods and services on the Internet.

Each other, One another
Each other refers to two persons or things.
*The interior and exterior colors complement **each other**.*

One another refers to more than two persons or things.
*Videoconferencing allows the diplomats to see **one another**.*

Eager, Anxious
*See entry for **Anxious, Eager**.*

Earthen, Earthly, Earthy
Earthen refers to being made of earth.
*Over the fire hangs a big **earthen** pot, the kind Indians used.*

Earthly refers to being of this world.
*Per his last request, his **earthly** remains were scattered at sea.*

Earthy refers to being down to earth, crude, or unrefined.
*The speaker's **earthy** expressions pleased the rebellious crowd.*

Eastward, Eastwards
Eastward is preferred in American usage.

Eclectic, Esoteric, Exoteric
Eclectic means the best of something from many sources.
*With music from Bach to the Beatles, the show was clearly **eclectic**.*

Esoteric means confined to or understood by just a few people.
The author's use of esoteric language can deter the reader.

Exoteric means suitable for all.
She designs and writes books for an exoteric audience.

Ecology, Environment

Ecology refers to relationships between organisms and their environment.
Last semester the class studied the ecology of the jungle.

Environment refers to conditions that surround an organism.
Many fear that nuclear waste can hurt our environment.

Economic, Economical

Economic refers to the economy, material wealth, or financial reward.
They predict a substantial economic recovery for next year.
We sold our Florida vacation house for economic reasons.

Economical refers to being not wasteful.
This car is more economical on gas than the others we tried.

Edition, Addition

See entry for Addition, Edition.

Eek, Eke

Eek is simply a noise one makes when frightened.
Eek! A bat just flew in their house.

Eke means to obtain something usually with difficulty.
For years he tried eking out a living on his low salary.

Eerie, Aerie, Airy

See entry for Aerie, Airy, Eerie.

Effect, Affect

See entry for Affect, Effect.

Effective, Effectual, Efficacious, Efficient

Effective means impressive, in effect, or producing a result.
*The band put on an **effective** performance at Saratoga.*
*The new fiscal calendar is **effective** as of next month.*
*The talks were **effective** in gaining peace within a few days.*

Effectual, like **effective**, means sufficient to produce a desired effect or result.
*"**Effectual** steps for the suppression of the rebellion."*—Macaulay

Efficacious means having the power to achieve the desired effect.
*The doctor discovered an **efficacious** remedy for the ailment.*

Efficient means achieving results from a good use of resources.
*Some fuel-**efficient** cars can get 60 miles to a gallon of gas.*

Effeminate, Feminine

Effeminate refers to a man with womanly traits.
*His long nails and long hair make him look **effeminate**.*

Feminine refers to characteristics of a woman or girl.
*The house colors would probably appeal to the **feminine** crowd.*

Effluent, Affluent

See entry for **Affluent, Effluent**.

Egress, Ingress

Egress refers to the legal right of a property owner *to leave* leased property. **Ingress** refers to the legal right of the property owner *to enter* leased property.

Egression, Aggression

See entry for **Aggression, Egression**.

Either, Neither

Either means one or the other but not both of two things.
*It's **either** higher taxes or some cutbacks.*

Neither means not one and not the other of two things.
*Under the new agreement, **neither** party may transfer its rights.*

Elapse, Lapse

Elapse means to pass by or slip away.
How much time elapses before the officials make a decision?

Lapse means to drift or discontinue.
The magazine subscription lapses unless you renew it soon.

Elegy, Eulogy

Elegy refers to a poem of lament or praise for a dead person.
Walt Whitman wrote a famous elegy on the death of Lincoln.

Eulogy refers to speech or writing in praise of someone, usually dead.
Earl Spencer wrote a moving eulogy to his sister, Princess Diana.

Elicit, Illegal, Illicit

Elicit means to bring out or draw forth.
The band's performances always elicit praise from the critics.

Illegal means unlawful.
It is illegal to use a handheld cell phone while driving.

Illicit means unlawful or prohibited.
The council fined the firm because of its illicit activities.

Eloquent, Articulate

See entry for Articulate, Eloquent.

Elude, Allude, Refer

See entry for Allude, Elude, Refer.

Elusive, Illusive

Elusive means hard to catch, grasp, or define.
Director Stanley Kubrick remained an elusive figure to the press.

Illusive means deceptive or unreal.
David Copperfield amazes audiences with his illusive magic tricks.

Embargo, Boycott

See entry for Boycott, Embargo.

Emend

Emend, Amend
See entry for **Amend, Emend**.

Emerge, Immerge, Immerse
Emerge means to come out, rise up, or come forth.
*More vacation time may **emerge** from the contract talks.*

Immerge and **immerse** mean to plunge into or submerge.
***Immerge** (**immerse**) the knee in ice to minimize the swelling.*

Emigrant, Immigrant, Migrant
Emigrant is one who leaves one's country to settle in another.
*The **emigrants** spent a few weeks aboard ship before landing.*

Immigrant is one who enters and settles in a new country.
*Many **immigrants** are looking for jobs in the metropolitan area.*

Migrant is one who travels about, especially in search of work.
*The **migrants** are working in the apple orchards of New York.*

Eminent, Immanent, Imminent
Eminent means distinguished, famous, or prominent.
***Eminent** scientists have serious concerns about the coral reefs.*

Immanent means inherent or present within the universe.
*The theologian suggests that God is **immanent** in all life forms.*

Imminent means about to happen or threatening.
*The bidders tell us the government contract award is **imminent**.*

Emollient, Emolument
Emollient refers to a softening, soothing, or less harsh effect.
*He took a more **emollient** approach than his harsh predecessor.*

Emolument refers to salary, wages, or perquisites.
*The **emolument** rate for late-night work will be increased.*

Empathy, Sympathy
Empathy is the ability to relate to someone.
*Having been poor as a child, Harry Chapin always had **empathy** for the hungry.*

Sympathy means feeling sorry for someone.
*The club conveyed its **sympathy** to the widow with a gift basket.*

Empirical, Imperial

Empirical means verifiable or provable by means of observation or experiment.
*No **empirical** evidence exists to suggest the accused was anywhere near the crime.*

Imperial means relating to or suggestive of an empire or a sovereign.
*Unfortunately, they acted on their **imperial** impulses and invaded the small country.*

Emulate, Simulate

Emulate means strive to equal or excel, usually through imitation.
*The new TV comedy tried to **emulate** another popular show.*

Simulate means to take on the appearance of something.
*The testing laboratory can **simulate** an actual aircraft landing.*

En route, On route

En route, meaning on the way, is the correct phrase.
*We were told the package is **en route** from the factory.*

Enclose, Inclose

Enclose is preferred in American usage.
*Please **enclose** your latest resume with the job application.*

Endemic, Epidemic

Endemic means peculiar to a given country or people.
*The fish are **endemic** to the waters of the Hawaiian Islands.*

An **epidemic** is something, usually a disease, that breaks out suddenly and affects many people.
*The polio **epidemic** still plagues some communities.*

Endless, Innumerable

Endless means without end, boundless, or interminable.
*The therapy prevents injury with an **endless** array of exercises.*

Innumerable means too many to count (countless).
*Yoga offers **innumerable** benefits to those seeking good health.*

Endnotes, Footnotes

Endnotes go at the *end* of chapters, and **footnotes** go at the *foot* (or bottom) of pages.

Enervate, Innervate, Invigorate

Enervate means to drain energy or weaken something.
*The continuous hot and humid weather **enervated** all of us.*

Innervate means to stimulate a nerve or muscle.
*Atrophy occurs when the cells that **innervate** the muscle die.*

Invigorate means to energize something.
*The brisk morning swim **invigorated** Harry and Greg.*

Enormity, Enormousness

Enormity means immensely outrageous or wicked.
*The **enormity** of the defendant's crimes surprised the entire jury.*

Enormousness refers to an object's large size.
*The **enormousness** of the new county facility amazed us.*

Enough, Ample

*See entry for **Ample, Enough**.*

Enquire, Inquire

Inquire is the preferred spelling, but either is acceptable.

Ensure, Assure, Insure

*See entry for **Assure, Ensure, Insure**.*

Enthral, Enthrall

Enthrall, meaning to captivate, is preferred in American usage.
*Tom's second spy novel **enthralled** us more than his first novel.*

Enthused, Enthusiastic

Enthused is not popular with writing experts. Use **enthusiastic**.
*The students are **enthusiastic** (not **enthused**) about the new school.*

Entitled, Titled

Entitled means to have the right to something.
*Because she is the songwriter, she is **entitled** to the royalties.*

Titled refers to the name of a publication, speech, or musical piece.
*Their first musical piece this evening is **titled**, "The Voice."*

Entomology, Etymology

Entomology is the study of insects. **Etymology** is the study of word origins.

Entrust, Intrust

Entrust is preferred in American usage.
*They **entrust** our firm with the management of their affairs.*

Enunciate, Annunciate

*See entry for **Annunciate, Enunciate**.*

Enure, Inure

Inure, meaning to get used to something undesirable, is preferred in American usage.
*We live in the woods, so we are **inured** to power outages.*

Envelop, Envelope

Envelop, a verb, means to enclose or surround.
*The mountain range was **enveloped** by raging fires last summer.*

Envelope, a noun, is the flat paper container for a letter.
*The special invitation arrived yesterday in a red **envelope**.*

Enviable, Envious

Enviable means worthy of envy.
*John Glenn has an **enviable** place in space travel history.*

Envious means showing envy.
*Some pilots are **envious** of John Glenn's mark on space travel.*

Envy, Jealousy

Envy means to desire something another person has and show resentment at the person having it.
*She gazed at his neighbor's house with **envy**.*

Jealousy is a resentful suspicion that someone else has what rightfully belongs to the **jealous** person.
*The favored treatment of the son created **jealousy** in the daughter.*

Epigram, Epigraph, Epitaph, Epithet

Epigram is a short humorous saying.
*Oscar Wilde wrote the **epigram**: "I can resist everything except temptation."*

Epigraph is a brief quotation at the beginning of a book or an inscription on a monument, statue, or building.
*The **epigraph** to E. M. Forster's novel* Howards End *is "Only connect!"*

Epitaph is a tribute to a dead person inscribed on a gravestone.
*A famous **epitaph** on a poker player's gravestone reads, "He played five aces, now he plays the harp."*

Epithet is a short descriptive word or phrase applied to a person.
*Bravery earned Richard Coeur de Lion the **epithet** 'Lionheart'.*

Equable, Equitable

Equable means unvarying, agreeable, or steady.
*Ireland's **equable** climate is due to its proximity to the sea.*

Equitable means impartial, fair, or reasonable.
*The club gave an **equitable** distribution of gifts to the charities.*

Equipment, Equipments

Use **equipment**. **Equipments** is not a word.

Equivocably, Equivocally

Equivocably is not a word.

Equivocate, Prevaricate, Procrastinate

Equivocate means to be deliberately ambiguous in order to mislead.
*He **equivocated** and gave complex answers to our questions.*

Prevaricate means to stray from the truth, mislead, or lie.
*He spoke with candor and saw no reason to **prevaricate**.*

Procrastinate means to postpone, put off, or defer.
*Why did the judges continue to **procrastinate** about a decision?*

Erasable, Irascible

Erasable means capable of being rubbed out or removed.
*Please use only **erasable** markers on the white marker boards.*

Irascible means disagreeable or easily provoked.
*After months of being unemployed, he became **irascible**.*

Erode, Corrode

*See entry for **Corrode, Erode**.*

Errant, Arrant

*See entry for **Arrant, Errant**.*

Errata, Erratum

Errata (plural form) refers to a publication's list of corrections
(e.g., *errata sheet*). **Erratum** is the singular form.

Eruption, Irruption

Eruption refers to a violent outburst or discharge of material.
*The **eruption** of Mount Vesuvius destroyed Pompei in 79 AD.*

Irruption refers to an increase, such as in population.
*An **irruption** of winter finches from the north woods is expected.*

Escape goat, Scapegoat

Scapegoat, which is one who is blamed for another's misdeeds,
is the correct word, though **escape goat** is actually closer to the
original meaning of the phrase. It has roots in an ancient Jewish
custom that allows one of two sacrificial goats to go free, taking
the sins of the people with it. This goat was the *escaped goat*,
which was later shortened to **scapegoat**.
*Making Jim the **scapegoat** for the team's loss is absurd.*

Esoteric, Exoteric

Esoteric means intended for a select few.
The author's esoteric use of language can deter the average reader.

Exoteric means not intended for a particular group but anyone.
Many books deal with the exoteric forms of the Egyptian mysteries.

Especially, Specially

Especially means particularly or standing apart from all the rest.
The air quality in the Adirondack Mountains is especially fresh.

Specially means for a specific purpose or reason.
Those students were specially chosen for their artistic talents.

Essay, Assay

See entry for Assay, Essay.

Eternity, Affinity, Infinity

See entry for Affinity, Eternity, Infinity.

Euphemism, Euphuism

Euphemism is an inoffensive word or phrase substituted for an offensive word or phrase.
The phrase "previously owned" is a euphemism for "used".

Euphuism is a style of prose from the Elizabethan period.
His writing style contrasts with the ornate style of euphuism.

Eurhythmic, Arrhythmic

See entry for Arrhythmic, Eurhythmic.

Evacuee, Refugee

Evacuee refers to a person removed from a dangerous area.
Many evacuees spent the night at a school during the storm.

Refugee refers to a person who flees for refuge or safety.
The refugee fled from the war and left his home country behind.

Eventually, Ultimately

Eventually means at an unspecified time in the future.
*Holly knew that **eventually** she would make the honor roll.*

Ultimately means at last or the end result of something.
***Ultimately**, they had to give in to the manager's request.*

Ever so often, Every so often

Ever so often means frequently; **every so often** means occasionally.
*Be sure to check (**ever so often**, or **every so often**) for news.*

Every body, Everybody

Every body means every person or thing without an exception.
***Every body** on the team will try to improve his or her golf swing.*

Everybody means all the people.
***Everybody** on the team knows Sam has the best golf swing.*

Every day, Everyday

Every day means each day without an exception.
*We try to back up our hard drive **every day**.*

Everyday means ordinary, common, or not unusual.
*Problems are a natural **everyday** occurrence of life.*

Every one, Everyone

Every one means every person or thing without an exception.
*To their dismay, the deer ate **every one** of the shrubs.*

Everyone means all the people.
*Is **everyone** ready to begin the meeting?*

Evidence, Proof

Evidence is information that helps form a conclusion.
*Scientists have **evidence** that life could have existed on Mars.*

Proof is factual information that verifies a conclusion.
*His attorney uncovered **proof** of Joe's innocence.*

Evident, Apparent

*See entry for **Apparent, Evident**.*

Evince, Evoke, Invoke

Evince means to exhibit or show something clearly.
*Paul McCartney **evinced** an amazing talent for music as a child.*

Evoke means to bring out something hidden or unexpressed.
*The music **evoked** many good memories of Molly's college days.*

Invoke means to call upon for help or to activate something.
*The defendant **invoked** the Fifth Amendment during the trial.*
*You can **invoke** that command by pressing the Enter key twice.*

Evocation, Avocation, Vocation

*See entry for **Avocation, Evocation, Vocation**.*

Ex-patriot, Expatriate

Expatriate is the correct word.

Exacerbate, Exasperate

Exacerbate means to make more violent, brutal, or severe.
*Closing the plant may **exacerbate** the bad mood in the town.*

Exasperate means to anger, irritate, or annoy.
*The voters were **exasperated** by the candidate's ignorance.*

Exaggerate, Overexaggerate

Overexaggerate is not a word. **Exaggerate** alone is sufficient.

Exalt, Exult

Exalt means to raise, praise, or elevate a person or thing.
*Let us **exalt** the brilliance of your achievements and ideas.*

Exult means to rejoice greatly.
*The professor **exulted** at being named department chairman.*

Exceed, Accede, Concede

*See entry for **Accede, Concede, Exceed**.*

Except, Accept
*See entry for **Accept, Except**.*

Exceptionable, Exceptional
Exceptionable means objectionable, offensive, or debatable.
*We found their crude language quite **exceptionable**.*
*The court made some **exceptionable** decisions today.*

Exceptional means uncommon, unusual, or extraordinary.
*That student has an **exceptional** memory for small details.*

Excess, Access
*See entry for **Access, Excess**.*

Exercise, Exorcize
Exercise means to use the mind or body in some activity.
*Jogging **exercises** the body as well as the mind.*

Exorcize means to drive out an evil spirit.
*The minister **exorcized** the house before the new owners moved in.*

Exhort, Extort
Exhort means to urge strongly or give warnings or advice.
*We are all **exhorted** therefore to live according to the law.*

Extort means to get something through force or intimidation.
*They were arrested for **extorting** money from the elderly.*

Exorbitant price, Exuberant price
Exorbitant price is the correct phrase.

Expand, Expend, Expound
Expand means to increase something.
*The company's healthcare business **expanded** by 50 percent.*

Expend means to lay out or spend.
*The company **expended** most of its effort on healthcare sales.*

Expound means to state in detail.
*The CPA **expounded** the intricacies of the new tax law.*

Expatiate, Expiate

Expatiate means to write or speak at great length.
*That company likes to **expatiate** in detail about its products.*

Expiate means to atone or make amends for something.
*He wanted to **expiate** the guilt he felt all those years.*

Expect, Anticipate

*See entry for **Anticipate, Expect**.*

*Mel **expended** all his money to **expand** his house.*

Expedient, Expeditious

Expedient means serving to promote or advance one's interest.
*It is **expedient** for him to start his re-election campaign early.*

Expeditious means acting with speed and efficiency.
*Please transfer the funds the most **expeditious** way.*

Explicit, Implicit

Explicit means clearly defined or stated.
*His surprising comments about the film are quite **explicit**.*

Implicit means implied or understood but not expressed.
*We have an **implicit** understanding with the building contractor.*

Expurgated, Abridged, Unabridged

*See entry for **Abridged, Expurgated, Unabridged**.*

Extant, Extent, Extinct

Extant means still existing.
*Few copies of Frank Sinatra's early albums are **extant**.*

Extent means the measure of or limit of something.
*We do not know the **extent** of the research done on the disease.*

Extinct means no longer in existence.
*Most of the animals that ever lived on earth are **extinct**.*

Extemporaneous, Impromptu, Spontaneous

Like the synonyms *improvised*, *ad hoc*, *ad lib*, *unrehearsed*, and
unplanned, these three words are also considered synonyms. The
exception may be with regard to speech making.

Extenuate, Attenuate

*See entry for **Attenuate, Extenuate**.*

Extrapolate, Interpolate

Extrapolate means to estimate or predict from known information.
*We can **extrapolate** from the data to determine an estimate.*

Interpolate means to insert something between other things.
*The editor's suggestions are **interpolated** clearly in the margins.*

Extrovert, Introvert

Extrovert refers to people who enjoy thrills with large groups of people. **Introvert** refers to people who enjoy calm activities with few people.

Eyelet, Islet

Eyelet is small hole edged with embroidered stitches as part of a design. **Islet** is a small island.

F

"All the fun's in how you say a thing."—Robert Frost

Fable, Legend, Myth, Parable

A **fable** is a simple, short, narrative story with animals as characters designed to enforce some useful truth or moral. A **legend** is an unverified story handed down from earlier times. A **myth** is a story usually dealing with a superhuman being and events that have no natural explanation. A **parable** also relates to a moral lesson, usually religious, and uses human characters to relay its message.

Facetious, Factious, Factitious

Facetious means humorous or flippant.
*Cathy was being **facetious** with her stories and meant no harm.*

Factious means causing internal dissension or opposition.
*A **factious** attitude can hinder any workplace.*

Factitious means artificial or unnatural.
*Speculation caused the **factitious** value of those stocks.*
*The doctor ruled out malingering or a **factitious** disorder.*

Facilitate, Felicitate

Facilitate means to make easier.
*His assistant **facilitates** the ordering process.*

Felicitate means to congratulate or make happy.
*The league **felicitated** Jon on his 100th game.*

Faint, Feign, Feint

Faint, as an adjective, refers to being dizzy, lacking clarity, or lacking brightness. As a verb, it means to lose consciousness.
*She suddenly felt **faint** after the rigorous workout in the gym.*
*He has a **faint** recollection of what happened last night.*
*The sun cast a **faint** shadow on the house at day's end.*
*Mom **fainted** when she learned about my award.*

Feign refers to giving a false appearance.
*In the driving class, one student was asked to **feign** an injury.*

Feint refers to giving a pretend punch in boxing.
*Muhammad Ali used many **feints** against his opponents.*

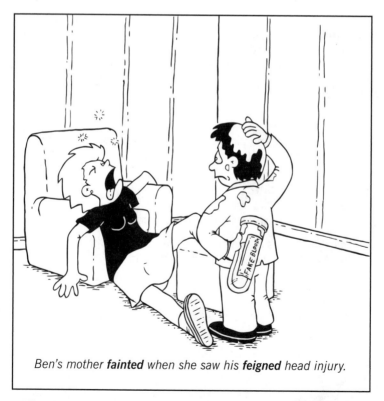

*Ben's mother **fainted** when she saw his **feigned** head injury.*

Fair to middling, Fair to midland

Fair to middling, meaning so-so, is the correct phrase. This late 1800s expression originally referred to cotton grading, where *fair* was one of the lowest grades of cotton and *middling* was the next lowest.

Famous, Infamous, Notorious

Famous means to be widely known.
*Tom Clancy, the **famous** author, autographed Eve's books.*

Infamous and **notorious** mean well known and unfavorably viewed.
*His philandering made him **infamous** (**notorious**) around town.*

Farther, Further

Farther refers to a physical distance.
*Do not place the unit **farther** than 10 feet from the house.*

Further refers to a greater degree or extent.
*Because of the legal aid ruling, the trial now faces **further** delay.*

Fatal, Fateful

Fatal refers to causing death, destruction, or ruin.
*By not heeding the advice, the group made a **fatal** mistake.*

Fateful refers to one's destiny.
*G. Lightfoot wrote about the Edmund Fitzgerald's **fateful** voyage.*

Father-in-laws, Fathers-in-law

Fathers-in-law is the correct phrase.

Faun, Fawn

Faun is a creature of Roman legend, part man and part goat.
*The **faun** is a disciple of the god Faunus.*

Fawn is a young deer usually less than a year old.
*If you see a **fawn** alone in a field, a doe is likely nearby.*

Faze, Phase

Faze means to disrupt or disturb something.
*The economic slowdown did not **faze** their business in any way.*

Phase, as a verb, means to carry out or conduct something. As a noun, **phase** is a stage of development.
*Mike is going to **phase** in the new procedures gradually.*
*The third **phase** of the building plan begins today.*

Fearful, Fearsome

Fearful means to be afraid of someone or something.
*They have grown more **fearful** about the year ahead.*

Fearsome means to cause fear in someone or something.
*A **fearsome** dog frightened the children.*

Feel, Believe, Think

*See entry for **Believe, Feel, Think**.*

Fell swoop, Foul swoop

Fell swoop, which means all at once or suddenly, is the correct phrase. Coined by Shakespeare in his 1605 play *Macbeth*, the phrase originally referred to a bird's rapid descent upon prey.
*In one **fell swoop**, she provided all the data the client needed.*

Feminine, Effeminate

*See entry for **Effeminate, Feminine**.*

Ferment, Foment

Ferment refers to commotion or unrest.
*The contest **fermented** much excitement from the crowd.*

Foment means to stir emotions or reactions, not necessarily bad.
*We do not want to **foment** any ill feeling.*

Note: In a totally different sense, the word *ferment* also relates to a substance capable of bringing about *fermentation*.

Fervent, Fervid

Fervent means passionate or warm.
*It is our **fervent** wish that Bob quickly recovers from his illness.*

Fervid means impassioned or extremely hot.
*Peggy and Joe have a **fervid** dislike for extremely cold climates.*
*They endured the **fervid** temperatures of the tropical climate.*

Fever, Temperature

*A person has a **fever** when his or her **temperature** is higher than 98.6° F.*

Few, Couple

*See entry for **Couple, Few**.*

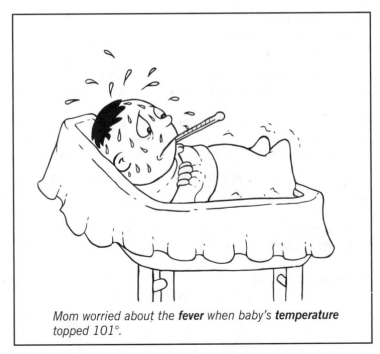

*Mom worried about the **fever** when baby's **temperature** topped 101°.*

Fewer, Less, Lest

Fewer refers to a number of individual persons or things.
Fewer than 50 applicants responded to the recent job vacancy.

Less refers to a quantity of something that cannot be counted as individual items.
Because of drought, the fields are producing less corn this year.

Note: If the number is only *one*, use **less**.
One less person attended the meeting.

Lest means for fear that.
Lest we forget, let's recognize Tom for his hard work right now.

Fiancé, Fiancée

Fiancé is a man engaged to be married. **Fiancée** is a woman engaged to be married.

Fictional, Fictitious

Fictional refers to fiction.
Yoda is a fictional character in "The Empire Strikes Back."

Fictitious refers to being imaginary or nonexistent.
They're conducting business under assumed or fictitious names.

Figuratively, Literally, Literately

Figuratively means metaphorically or symbolically.
Figuratively speaking, it is turning the business world on edge.

Literally means following the exact meanings of the words.
Several community volunteers literally built that house in two months.

Literately is an adverb referring to the ability to read and write.
We helped the literately impaired people learn the latest news.

Filipinos, Philippinos

People of the Philippines are referred to as **Filipinos**.

First, Firstly

First, an adverb, does not need an *ly*.
First (not firstly), we could consider an alternative method.

Note: This advice also applies to *secondly, thirdly, lastly,* etc.

First come - first serve, First come - first served

First come – first served is the correct phrase.

Fiscal, Monetary

Fiscal applies to budgetary matters, and **monetary** applies to money supply.

Flagrant, Blatant

*See entry for **Blatant, Flagrant**.*

Flair, Flare

Flair refers to a natural ability or aptitude to do something.
*She has a natural talent and **flair** for performing on stage.*

Flare refers to a bright light or flame.
*The police set up a road **flare** around the accident.*

Flambé, Flambeau

Flambé refers to food served with flaming liquor, and a **flambeau** is a large ornamental candlestick.

Flammable, Inflammable, Nonflammable

Flammable and **inflammable** are synonyms meaning burnable.
*Never light a match near a **flammable (inflammable)** liquid.*

Nonflammable means not flammable or not easily ignited.
*Trichlorofluoro methane is a colorless, **nonflammable** gas.*

Flatus, Afflatus

Flatus refers to gas generated by the intestine, and **afflatus** refers to divine inspiration.

Flaunt, Flout

Flaunt means to display boastfully or show off something.
*They **flaunt** their wealth by driving expensive cars to school.*

Flout means to ignore or show disrespect for rules.
*The haughty teens **flout** the most basic school rules.*

Flesh out, Flush out

Flesh out means to expand or give substance to something (e.g., *plan* or *idea*).
*He promised to **flesh out** the details of his reorganization next week.*

Flush out means to force someone or something out of hiding or to clean something (usually with water).
*The police fired tear gas to **flush out** the criminals.*
*He used green tea and a lot of water to **flush out** his system.*

Flood, Deluge

A **flood** is overflowing water that covers land. It typically leaves damage. A **deluge** is a large, heavy downpour of water that typically does not leave damage.

Florescent, Fluorescent

Florescent means a time of blossoming or flowering.
*His recent accolades indicate a **florescent** career in industry.*

Fluorescent means giving off light from radiation.
*Often **florescent** lights are used in greenhouses.*

Flotsam, Jetsam

Flotsam is floating cargo or wreckage following a shipwreck.
*The **flotsam** floated for weeks, long after the ship sank.*

Jetsam is something thrown overboard to lighten a ship in distress.
*The **jetsam** consisted of many cartons of canned food.*

Flounder, Founder

Flounder means to behave awkwardly or move in a clumsy way.
*The key witness **floundered** during her testimony.*
*Art **floundered** a minute on the ice before gaining his balance.*

Founder means to sink or collapse.
*On its approach, the boat struck a reef and quickly **foundered**.*
*The prosecutor's case **foundered** after a key witness' testimony.*

Footnotes, Endnotes

Footnotes go at the *foot* (or bottom) of pages, and **endnotes** go at the *end* of chapters.

Forbear, Forebear

Forbear, a verb, means to abstain or refrain from something.
*We **forbear** from making any negative comments about them.*

Forebear, a noun, means an ancestor.
*One of my **forebears** came to America on the Mayflower.*

Forbid, Prohibit

Both these verbs mean to disallow something.

Forbid is usually used in cases of more personal situations.
*Their coach **forbids** them missing any Saturday practice.*

Prohibit is usually used in cases of lawful situations.
*The school **prohibits** them from leaving the grounds at lunch.*

Forbidding, Foreboding

Forbidding means unpleasant, often with the connotation something is being prevented or slowed.
*He gave us a **forbidding** look when we asked about our bill.*
*The **forbidding** traffic made us late for the game.*

Foreboding is a premonition about something (usually negative).
*She had a **foreboding** her husband would be injured on the job.*

Forceful, Forcible

Forceful means powerful, vigorous, or effective.
*His **forceful** personality dominates much of the interview.*

Forcible means exercising by force or violence.
*The firefighters made a **forcible** entry into the burning building.*

Forego, Forgo

Forego means to go before in place or time.
*Her competent work and reputation always **forego** her.*
*It is a **foregone** conclusion that John will retire this year.*

Forgo means to give up, do without, or relinquish something.
*To compete in running races, you should **forgo** fatty foods.*

Foreword, Introduction, Preface

The **foreword** (not *forward*) of a book is a short note at the beginning of a book that usually tells us how the book originated. Alternately, a **foreword** is a short introductory note written by someone other than the author. The **preface** is a statement written by the author about the book's objective or purpose. An **introduction**, which can be written by the author or another person, follows the foreword and preface and tells the reader what to expect in the book.

Forgetful, Oblivious

Forgetful refers to a tendency not to remember.
*We found that **forgetful** behavior is common after the illness.*

Oblivious refers to being unaware or unmindful of something.
*They are **oblivious** that cameras are filming them.*

Formally, Formerly

Formally means in a traditional or formal manner.
*Celeste and Daniel are dressed **formally** for the occasion.*

Formerly means in the past.
*Jesse Ventura was **formerly** known as "The Body".*

Former, Latter

Former refers to the first of two and **latter** the second of two (or last of many). Note that when you use these words, the reader must remember what was written. This can sometimes be annoying, so you might want to reconsider using these words.

Formula, Formulae, Formulas

Formula is the singular form and **formulae** and **formulas** are the plural forms (**formulas** is more common).
*We're applying geometric **formulas** for finding the area.*

Forte, Forte

Two **fortes** in English exist, but today both have the same pronunciation (*for-tay*).

Forte has Italian word roots and is used in a musical context.
*Try to play the measure **forte**.*

Forte has French word roots and refers to a strong point or strength.
*Carpentry is not my **forte** around the house.*

Fortuitous, Fortunate

Fortuitous means happening by chance or randomly, often with a positive connotation.
*The **fortuitous** software sales caused a rise in revenue.*

Fortunate means being lucky or having good fortune.
*She is **fortunate** in that her unemployment lasted just a few months.*

Forward, Forwards

Forward means to be toward the front or to send on.
*Please step **forward** when your name is called.*
*Please **forward** the bill to the customer's new home address.*

Forwards is not preferred in American usage. Use **forward** instead.

Fragment, Fragmentary

Fragment refers to a small part detached from something.
*That meteorite may be a **fragment** of a primitive asteroid.*

Fragmentary refers to disconnected or incomplete parts.
*It is possible to reconstruct organisms from **fragmentary** remains.*

Frantically, Franticly

Frantically is preferred in American usage.

Free, Freely

Free means without charge.
*Both faculty and students are admitted to the game **free**.*

Freely, an adverb, means in a free manner or without any restrictions.
*They **freely** voiced their opinions to their boss.*

Freeze, Frieze

Freeze means to change a liquid into a solid, to stop, or to exclude.
*Salt water **freezes** at a lower temperature than pure water.*
*When I access the Internet, my computer tends to **freeze**.*
*The higher park fees could **freeze** out the lower income families.*

Frieze refers to an ornament.
*A **frieze** that shows the history of the city is hung in the hallway.*

Friend, Acquaintance

A **friend** is a person one knows, likes, and trusts. An **acquaintance** is a person one knows.
*Joe is an example of an **acquaintance** who became a **friend**.*

Frontward, Frontwards

Frontward is preferred in American usage.

Fulsome, Abundant

*See entry for **Abundant, Fulsome**.*

Funeral, Funerary, Funereal

Funeral refers to the service held for a dead person.
*The **funeral** was a celebration of his life.*

Funerary means associated with burial.
*The anthropologist studied the **funerary** beliefs of 500 years ago.*

Funereal means like a funeral, suggestive of death, gloomy, or sad.
*Where earlier the tone was quite **funereal**, now it feels uplifting.*

Fungous, Fungus

Fungous is the adjective (***fungous** diseases of plants*), and **fungus** is the noun (***fungus** can grow in damp environments*).

G

"When ideas fail, words come in very handy."—Johann Wolfgang von Goethe

Gabardine, Gaberdine

Gabardine, a durable fabric with a twill weave, is preferred in American usage.
*Daniel is wearing his blue **gabardine** slacks to the interview.*

Gaff, Gaffe

Gaff is an iron hook attached to a pole usually used to grab large fish.
*The seaman uses a **gaff** to pull in the large tuna.*

Gaffe is a social error, blunder, or indiscreet remark (faux pas).
*I made a **gaffe** by mispronouncing my supervisor's last name.*

Gait, Gate

Gait means to trot or canter.
*The crowd watched the horse's **gait** carefully.*

Gate is an entrance or exit.
*Once you enter the code, the **gate** will automatically open.*

Gallop, Galop

Gallop refers to a fast gait or doing something quickly. **Galop** is an old word that refers to a lively dance.

Gambit, Gamut

Gambit is an opening maneuver or remark to gain an advantage.
*Her clever opening **gambit** gave her quite an advantage.*

Gamut is a full range of something.
*That book runs the **gamut** of golf swing tips.*

Gamble, Gambol

Gamble means to risk, chance, or bet on something.
*I would not **gamble** my rent money at the casino.*

To **gambol** means to leap and skip about playfully.
*The children are joyfully **gamboling** around the school yard.*

Gantlet, Gauntlet

Gantlet, an old form of punishment, requires a person to run between two lines of people who flog him as he passes.
*Thieves were once made to run the **gantlet** as their punishment.*

Gauntlet refers to a heavy armored glove worn in medieval times. It is often used figuratively to mean a challenge, as in *he threw down the **gauntlet***.

Garnish, Garnishee

Garnish means to enhance in appearance or decorate something (most commonly food).
*His broad-toed shoes were **garnished** with gold buckles.*
*The plate was **garnished** with a parsley sprig.*

Garnishee, a legal term, means to seize one's property or money.
*The loan company **garnisheed** the deadbeat's wages.*

Gazetteer, Atlas

A **gazetteer** is a geographical dictionary or index usually found at the back of an **atlas,** and an **atlas** is a bound map collection.

Gel, Jell

Gel is the liquid one uses to style hair.
Gel can be especially useful for wavy and curly hair.

Jell means to take shape and become cohesive.
*Because of the players' inexperience, the team has yet to **jell**.*

Gender, Sex

Gender describes the characteristics that a society or culture delineates as masculine or feminine. **Sex** refers to biological differences: chromosomes, hormonal profiles, and internal and external sex organs.

123

Genial, Congenial, Congenital
*See entry for **Congenial, Congenital, Genial**.*

Genius, Genus
Genius is a person with exceptional ability, intelligence, or talent.
*Surprisingly, Albert Einstein was not considered a boy **genius**.*

Genus is a category, class, or type in taxonomy.
*The museum lists all the plants by both **genus** and species.*

Genteel, Gentile
Genteel means well mannered and refined.
*She encouraged her daughter to behave in a **genteel** fashion.*

Gentile refers to a person of non-Jewish faith.
*The ceremonial laws excluded the **Gentiles** from being the people of God.*

Gesture, Jester
Gesture refers to moving various body parts (hands, arms, etc.) to communicate.
*The baseball umpire used a common **gesture** to show the runner was safe.*

Jester refers to someone acting in a foolish manner.
*In medieval times, **jesters** typically entertained guests and royalty.*

Get my dander up, Get my dandruff up
Get my dander up is the correct expression. It means angry, and originates from the 1800s Dutch phrase *op donderon*, which means to burst into a sudden rage.
*Those needless delays at the airport really **get my dander up**.*

Gibe, Jibe
Gibe means to jeer, mock, or tease a person.
*Eric sometimes **gibes** him about his unfortunate four-putt green.*

Jibe means to agree with something.
*Her independent audit **jibes** well with our accounting numbers.*

Gild, Guild

Gild means to cover with a golden appearance.
*The beautiful Canadian sunset **gilded** the grass in the valley.*

Guild refers to an association of trades people.
*Steven Spielberg is a member of the Directors **Guild** of America.*

Gilt, Guilt

Gilt, as an adjective, means covered with gold (from the verb *gild*).
*She is wearing an elaborate **gilt** necklace to the party.*

Gilt, as a noun, refers to a thin gold covering or layer.
*Over the years much of the **gilt** wore away from the necklace.*

Guilt, a noun, is the responsibility for a wrongdoing or error.
*The prosecutor proved the accused's **guilt** in the crime.*

Gist, Jest

Gist refers to the central idea of something.
*I understand the **gist** of what Tommy is trying to say.*

Jest refers to a joke.
*I spoke in **jest**, but Jane was offended by my comments.*

Glacier, Glazier

Glacier is a large body of ice found on a hillside or mountain.
*The **glacier** moved slowly down the hillside and into the ocean.*

Glazier is one who cuts glass especially for doors and windows.
*The **glazier** promptly repaired the broken window.*

Gluten, Glutton

Gluten is a protein substance found in corn and wheat cereal grains.
*A strict **gluten**-free diet can improve a person's health.*

Glutton is someone who eats or drinks to excess, or someone who has a great capacity for enduring something.
*"I am not a **glutton**. I am an explorer of food."*—Erma Bombeck
*You must be a **glutton** for pain to run another marathon.*

Goggle, Google, Googol

Goggle means to look at something in amazement or surprise.
*The huge statue of the Virgin Mary caused him to **goggle** in amazement.*

Google is the name of the search engine and software company. The name is an intentional variant of the mathematical term **googol**, which equals 10^{100}.

Gone, Went

Gone must always be preceded by 1 of the 23 auxiliary (or helping) verbs (*are*, *was*, *were*, *have*, and others). **Went** never takes an auxiliary (or helping) verb.
*I should **have gone** to college when I had the chance.*
*I **went** to college immediately after high school.*

Note: The 23 auxiliary (or helping) verbs are: *am*, *are*, *be*, *being*, *been*, *can*, *could*, *did*, *do*, *does*, *had*, *has*, *have*, *is*, *may*, *might*, *must*, *shall*, *should*, *was*, *were*, *will*, and *would*.

Good, Well

Good is an adjective.
*Debbie has always been a **good** elementary teacher.*

Well can be an adjective (referring to one's health) or an adverb.
*A few of the students do not look **well** today.*
*Debbie has always taught the students **well**.*

Gored, Gourd

Gored refers to piercing, stabbing, or wounding with a pointed instrument (spear). **Gourd** refers to any of numerous hard-rinded inedible fruits.

Gorilla, Guerrilla

Gorilla refers to a large ape. **Guerrilla** refers to a member (soldier) of an independent armed resistance force.

Gourmand, Gourmet

Gourmand refers to someone who is fond of food and drink.
*Brian is quite a **gourmand** and never skimps in his shopping.*

Gourmet refers to a connoisseur of fine food and drink.
*Being a **gourmet** is one requirement for a TV cooking expert.*

Graduated, Graduated from

Graduated from is the correct phrase.
*With high honors, I **graduated from** the University at Albany.*

Grammar, Syntax

Grammar is the complete study of a language. **Syntax** is a part of grammar that deals with how words form phrases, clauses, and sentences.

*The **guerrilla** warily eyed the **gorilla**.*

Grateful, Gratified, Gratuitous

Grateful means to feel gratitude.
*Many parents are **grateful** for the principal's intervention.*

Gratified means to give pleasure or satisfy.
*Walter's achievements in high school **gratified** his parents.*

Gratuitous means free, unjustified, or unwanted.
*His **gratuitous** advice on writing bored the veteran journalists.*

Great Britain, British Isles, United Kingdom

See entry for **British Isles, Great Britain, United Kingdom**.

Greave, Grieve

Greave is the medieval piece of armor covering the lower leg.
*Before battle, the **greave** was fastened to the knight's leg.*

Grieve means to cause distress or sorrow.
*When notified of his termination, he began to **grieve**.*

Grisly, Gristly, Grizzled, Grizzly

Grisly means ghastly or gruesome.
*The prosecutor painted a **grisly** picture of the event.*

Gristly means composed of or containing gristle.
*The children gave the dog the **gristly** end to chew.*

Grizzled means partly gray or streaked with gray.
*Our leader today is a **grizzled** veteran of many mountain climbs.*

Grizzly is a bear.
*The **grizzly** bear is the greatest symbol of the wilderness.*

Guarantee, Guaranty

Guarantee, a noun or verb, refers to assurance or security.
*The store offers a one-year **guarantee** on the used appliance.*
*The manufacturer **guarantees** the stove for one year.*

Guaranty, a noun, also means assurance or security.
*The salesperson's record is a **guaranty** of his honesty with clients.*

H

"A word is not a crystal, transparent and unchanging. It is the skin of living thought."—Oliver Wendell Holmes, Jr.

Habitant, Habitat, Inhabitant

Habitant and **inhabitant** both mean a person or animal who lives in a given area.
*Few **habitants** (**inhabitants**) of that area escaped the storm.*

Habitat is the environment of a person, animal, or plant.
*Johnny supports organizations that conserve **habitat** for wildlife.*

Had ought to, ought to

Had ought to is incorrect. Just the phrase **ought to** is sufficient.
*He **ought to** have gone to the party instead of staying home.*

Hairbrained, Harebrained

The correct word is **harebrained**, meaning having no more sense than a *hare* (rabbit).

Half-mast, Half-staff

Half-mast refers to a flag's position when flown on ships or at Naval stations. **Half-staff** refers to a flag's position when flown ashore.

Handsome, Hansom

Handsome means dignified in appearance or being generous.
*He looked **handsome** in his new Easter outfit.*
*A **handsome** reward is being offered for the dog's return.*

Hansom is a two-wheeled horse-drawn covered carriage with the driver's seat above and behind the passengers.
*They took a ride throughout the village in an old **hansom**.*

Hangar, Hanger

A **hangar** is a building that houses things like airplanes, and a **hanger** is a device used for hanging items like clothes.

Hanged, Hung

Hanged means executed by hanging.
*The five conspirators in the Lincoln assassination were **hanged**.*

Hung means suspended.
*The Christmas stockings are **hung** by the chimney with care.*

Note: Some word authorities accept **hung** as meaning executed.

Hapless, Hopeless

Hapless refers to being unlucky or always experiencing unfortunate things.
*It was heart breaking to see the **hapless** flood victims.*

Hopeless refers to despair or simply having no hope at all (a pessimist).
*What appeared **hopeless**, we now see light at the end of the tunnel.*

Hara-kiri, Kamikaze

Hara-kiri is Japanese suicide by slitting the belly, and **Kamikaze** is Japanese suicide by crashing an aircraft on the enemy.

Harbinger, Harbringer

Harbinger is the correct word.

Harbor, Port

A **harbor** is a body of water that protects ships. A **port** is a place where ships load and unload their cargo.

Hardly than, Hardly when

Hardly when is the correct expression.
***Hardly** had the surgeons opened me **when** my aorta ruptured.*

Hardy, Hearty

Hardy means courageous, daring, or capable of withstanding tough conditions.
*Unlike tender plants, some **hardy** plants can survive freezing temperatures.*

Hearty means showing heartfelt affection or providing abundant nourishment.
*He spoke of his late wife with the most **hearty** affection.*
*Some researchers feel a **hearty** breakfast can help one lose weight.*

Harebrained, Hairbrained

The correct word is **harebrained**, meaning having no more sense than a *hare* (rabbit).

Hark, Hawk, Hock

Hark means to pay close attention.
Hark, the store will open for Christmas shopping at 5 a.m.

Hawk means to sell something.
*We saw street vendors **hawking** luggage to many people.*

Hock means to pawn or trade something.
*She had to **hock** her diamond to pay her medical bills.*

Hate, Despise

*See entry for **Despise, Hate**.*

Have, Of

Have is an auxiliary verb that is used with *could*, *must*, *should*, *would*, *may*, and *might*.
*The meeting with the CEO **must have** been interesting.*

Of is a simple preposition that is usually preceded by a noun.
*One **of** us made a mistake in predicting the outcome.*

Healthful, Healthy

Healthful means conducive to good health.
*Because of its **healthful** climate, we chose to live there all year.*

Healthy means possessing good health.
*Diet, exercise, and rest keep them **healthy** and energetic.*

Memory hook: Things are **healthful**; people and animals are **healthy**.

Hear, hear/Here, here

Hear, hear, an expression indicating approval, is the correct phrase.

Hear, Listen

Hear means to be aware of sounds in your ears.
*Can you **hear** me over there despite all the noise?*

Listen means to pay attention to something you can *hear*. You usually need the preposition *to* with it.
*Try to **listen** to what the instructor has to say about the test.*

Heart-rendering, Heart-rending

Heart-rending is the correct phrase.
*It's definitely one of the most **heart-rending** films we've seen.*

Height, Heighth

The correct spelling today is **height**, though years ago the word ended in *th*.

Hemiplegic, Paraplegic, Quadriplegic

Hemiplegic means being paralyzed on one side of the body; **paraplegic** means being paralyzed in the lower half of the body (including the legs); **quadriplegic** means being paralyzed on all four limbs.

Hence, Thence, Whence

Hence means from here, from now, or thus.
*Two years **hence** this entire episode will be forgotten by all.*
*It is going to rain, **hence** the high humidity and clouds.*

Thence means from that time or from that place.
*We flew to Raleigh and **thence** to Dallas on our way back.*

Whence (an old word) means from what place, source, or cause.
***Whence** came all this valuable information?*

Herbivorous, Carnivorous, Omnivorous

*See entry for **Carnivorous, Herbivorous, Omnivorous**.*

Hereafter, Hereinafter

Hereafter means life after death or in the future.
*Belief in the **hereafter** is a fundamental part of their faith.*
*The group must comply with all present and **hereafter** regulations.*

Hereinafter means in the following part of a document.
*The Value-Added Tax (**hereinafter** referred to as VAT) will
increase next year.*

Herein, Herewith

Both words are business jargon and should be avoided in writing.
*They have **enclosed** (not **herein** or **herewith**) receipts for all
travel expenses.*

Heritage, Hermitage

Heritage refers to inherited property, status acquired through
birth, or a tradition. **Hermitage** refers to a place where one can
live in seclusion (an abbey or monastery).

Heroin, Heroine

Heroin is a drug. **Heroine** is the principal female character in a
novel, poem, or drama. It can also refer to a woman noted for
courage, daring action, or special achievement.

Hew, Hue

Hew means to cut or chop using a sharp instrument (e.g., *axe*).
*The fire fighters used an axe to **hew** the dead trees from the forest.*

Hue is a gradient of color that helps to classify other colors.
*We picked a blue **hue** of paint to match the living room chairs.*

Hilarious, Hysterical

Hilarious refers to something (not a person) being very funny.
*The film was simply **hilarious**.*

Hysterical refers to people when they lose control of their emotions.
*We laughed **hysterically** at the film.*

Hinder, Prevent

Hinder means to delay, impede, or make things difficult.
*The leg cast may **hinder** some of her movements.*

Prevent means to stop something from happening or succeeding.
*If you take precautions, you will **prevent** an accident.*

Hippie, Hippy

Hippie is a long-haired flower child from the 1960s, and **hippy** is an adjective that describes a person with wide hips.

Historic, Historical

Historic refers to something important or memorable.
*The opening of the wing is a **historic** occasion for the hospital.*

Historical means concerned with or relating to history.
*Margaret Mitchell's "Gone with the Wind" is a **historical** novel.*

Hoard, Horde

Hoard refers to a hidden find or cache.
*Jim found a **hoard** of Roman coins with his metal detector.*

Horde refers to a crowd or throng.
*We ran into a **horde** of mosquitoes at last night's softball game.*

Hoi polloi, Hoity-toity

Hoi polloi means the common people or the masses.
*We were delighted to see their heroes riding with the **hoi polloi**.*

Hoity-toity means the elite, snobbish, or the upper class.
*You'll never catch us hanging out with a **hoity-toity** crowd.*

Home, House

Home refers to intangible things (emotions) within a dwelling.
*It's obvious they are all being raised in a very happy **home**.*

House refers to a structure that can be built, bought, or sold.
*The real estate broker just put her **house** on the market.*

Home in on, Hone in on

Home in on, meaning to aim at a target, is the correct phrase.
*With that obvious clue, we can quickly **home in on** the answer.*

Homogeneous, Homogenous

Homogeneous means of the same or similar nature or kind.
*It was a **homogeneous** club, its members having similar values.*

Homogenous means resembling in structure, due to descent.
*As shown by their like physiology, the animals are **homogenous**.*

*The **horde** of miners found a **hoard** of gold coins.*

Homographs, Homonyms, Homophones

Homographs are words spelled alike but different in meaning and pronunciation (noun *project* vs. the verb *project*).

Homonyms are words spelled and pronounced alike but have different meanings (A *bear* can *bear* very cold temperatures.).

Homophones are words pronounced alike but different in spelling and meaning (*their, there* and *real, reel*).

Honorarium, Stipend

Honorarium is a gift of payment for a service instead of a set price.
*They gave Kerry an **honorarium** for his architecture advice.*

Stipend is an agreed to sum of money for a periodic service.
*She gets a large **stipend** from the college every three months.*

Hostel, Hostile

Hostel refers to an inexpensive hotel usually for young travelers.
*Pete reserved his **hostel** online to ensure he had a place to stay.*

Hostile refers to being exceptionally unfriendly or antagonist.
*The **hostile** forces failed to sabotage the revolution.*

How ever, However

How ever is used for emphasis.
***How ever** did you get front row seats for the concert?*

However means in whatever manner or nevertheless.
***However** the board decides, we probably should just accept it.*
***However,** the board should make a decision on the matter soon.*

Hue, Shade, Tint

Hue is a color's intensity. **Shade** is a degree of darkness of a color. **Tint** is a pale variation of a color.

Humerus, Humorous

Humerus is the long bone of the upper arm that extends from the shoulder to the elbow. **Humorous** means being funny or amusing.

Hurdle, Hurtle

Hurdle refers to a difficulty or obstacle.
*The Health Care Bill cleared a big **hurdle** in the Senate today.*

Hurtle means to move with great speed or to go violently.
*Many baby boomers are **hurtling** toward their retirement age.*
*The tornado sent debris **hurtling** all over the community.*

Hurricane, Typhoon

A **hurricane** is a severe tropical storm that starts east of the International Date Line (Atlantic Ocean, Caribbean Sea, or Gulf of Mexico). A **typhoon** is a severe tropical storm that starts west of the International Date Line (Pacific Ocean or China Sea).

Hypercritical, Hypocritical

Hypercritical means over critical, excessively exact, or picky.
*His **hypercritical** movie review has the producers concerned.*

Hypocritical means two-faced or practicing hypocrisy.
*It is **hypocritical** of the newspaper to criticize the paparazzi.*

Hyperthermia, Hypothermia

Hyperthermia refers to an elevated body temperature when the body produces or absorbs more heat than it can dissipate. **Hypothermia** is just the opposite; the core temperature drops below that required for normal metabolism and body functions.

I

"Half my life is an act of revision."—John Irving

Ice tea, Iced tea
Iced tea is the correct phrase.

If I was, If I were
If I were is the correct phrase when one is referring to a conditional future event.
If I were president, I would stress feeding the hungry.

Ignorant, Stupid
Ignorant means not having learned.
*They tend to assume that people in earlier times were **ignorant**.*

Stupid means not able to learn.
*The worker was uneducated, but not necessarily **stupid**.*

Illegal, Illicit, Elicit
*See entry for **Elicit, Illegal, Illicit**.*

Illegible, Unreadable
Illegible means impossible to read because the words cannot be made out.
*For me, not the pharmacist, the prescription is **illegible**.*

Unreadable means the material is uninteresting or poorly written.
*The grammatical errors made the letter simply **unreadable**.*

Illiterate, Alliterate
*See entry for **Alliterate, Illiterate**.*

Illusion, Delusion, Allusion
*See entry for **Allusion, Delusion, Illusion**.*

Illusive, Elusive
*See entry for **Elusive, Illusive**.*

Imaginary, Imaginative
Imaginary means not real.
Imaginary friends are typical for kids between ages 3 and 6.

Imaginative means to show an imagination.
*Jim Henson's **imaginative** ability brought joy to many families.*

Immanent, Imminent, Eminent
*See entry for **Eminent, Immanent, Imminent**.*

Immature, Premature
Immature means not developed or fully grown.
*That child appears **immature** compared to the rest of the class.*

Premature means before the expected time (too soon).
*The **premature** infant was born at only seven months.*

Immemorial, Immortal, In memoriam
Immemorial means ancient beyond memory.
*His family had farmed that land since time **immemorial**.*

Immortal means deathless or eternal.
*In literature, Shakespeare is a true **immortal**.*

In memoriam means in memory of (obituary).

Immerge, Immerse, Emerge
*See entry for **Emerge, Immerge, Immerse**.*

Immigrant, Emigrant, Migrant
*See entry for **Emigrant, Immigrant, Migrant**.*

Immoral, Amoral
*See entry for **Amoral, Immoral**.*

Immunity, Impunity

Immunity means exempt from disease or obligation.
*The new vaccine provides **immunity** against chicken pox.*
*The church was granted **immunity** from any local taxation.*

Impunity means exempt from harm, penalty, or punishment.
*The favorite child teased his brother with **impunity**.*

Immure, Inure

Immure means to enclose within, imprison, or confine.
*She locked all the doors and **immured** herself in the house.*

Inure means to get used to something difficult, painful, or unpleasant.
*He has become **inured** to the difficulty of the English language.*

Impartable, Impartible

Impartable means capable of being transmitted, communicated, or shared.
*The blacksmith's knowledge is **impartable**, if only we listen.*

Impartible means not divisible or not subject to partition.
*The children were sad to learn their father's estate is **impartible**.*

Impassable, Impassible

Impassable means not passable or cannot be traveled over.
*The road is **impassable** in winter and early spring.*

Impassible, a theological term, means incapable of suffering.
*He believes God does not suffer and is therefore **impassible**.*

Impel, Induce

Impel means to force an action.
*Factories are **impelled** to follow the environmental regulations.*

Induce means to persuade or to cause to do something.
*The doctor prescribed a mild drug to **induce** sleep.*

Imperial, Empirical

See entry for **Empirical, Imperial**.

Impertinence, Pertinence

Impertinence means to be rude.
*His **impertinence** in class wasted valuable time.*

Pertinence means having logical precise relevance to the matter at hand.
*The memorial has particular **pertinence** to the victim's families.*

Impetuous, Impetus

Impetuous means acting impulsively or rashly.
*The **impetuous** person spent all his money carelessly.*

Impetus means the force or momentum to achieve something.
*Per the schedule, an **impetus** to move the idea forward exists.*

Implicit, Explicit

*See entry for **Explicit, Implicit**.*

Imply, Infer

Imply means to convey or suggest a meaning indirectly.
*Her memo **implies** that the project would be delayed a week.*

Infer means to conclude from facts or premises.
*She **infers** from the evidence that the accused is not guilty.*

Memory hook: Speakers and writers **imply**; listeners and readers **infer**.

Impostor, Imposture

An **impostor** is a person who pretends to be someone else.
*The **impostor** felt he could bluff his way through the checkpoint.*

Imposture is the act of deception.
*Laws exist against the **imposture** of hyping worthless stocks.*

Impracticable, Impractical

Impracticable means not capable of being done.
*The extensive damage made repairing the car **impracticable**.*

Impractical means having little practical value.
*A plan for a new stadium would be seen as **impractical**.*

Impromptu, Extemporaneous, Spontaneous

See entry for **Extemporaneous, Impromptu, Spontaneous**.

Impulsive, Compulsive, Compulsory

See entry for **Compulsive, Compulsory, Impulsive**.

In depth, Indepth

In depth is always two words.
*Let us take an **in depth** look at news stories.*

In fact, Infact

In fact is always two words.
In fact, it's a surprise the team scores as well as it does.

In regard to, In regards to

In regard to, without an *s*, is the correct phrase. Sometimes you can avoid this phrase by substituting words like *on*, *about*, or *concerning*.
*He notified us **in regard to** (on, about, concerning) the change.*

In tact, Intact

Intact is always one word.

In the fact that, By the fact that

See entry for **By the fact that, In the fact that**.

In the same vane, In the same vein

In the same vein, which means similar or on the same topic, is the correct phrase.
*Author Jack Higgins writes **in the same vein** as Ian Fleming.*

Inalienable, Unalienable

Either word is correct, but **inalienable** is more common today.

Inanition, Inanity

Inanition is a lack of vitality or spirit, or exhaustion from hunger.
*The cheerleaders' **inanition** irritated the basketball coach.*
*The report details how the prisoners were starved into **inanition**.*

Inanity means a total lack of meaning, ideas, or sense.
*He resented the **inanity** of the tasks given to him daily.*

Inapt, Inept

Inapt means inappropriate or unsuitable.
*The only flaw in the film is an **inapt** and annoying soundtrack.*

Inept means awkward, clumsy, or uncoordinated.
*His **inept** words during the speech made him look incompetent.*

Incident, Accident, Mishap

*See entry for **Accident, Incident, Mishap**.*

Incidentally, Incidently

Incidentally means by chance or not intentionally. The word is
commonly used to indicate that something is related, but not
pertinent, to a topic being discussed.
*We like cheese. **Incidentally**, cheese has lots of calcium.*

Incidently is not a word.

Incipient, Insipid, Insipient

Incipient means emerging, developing, or vital.
*During the exam, the doctor recognized an **incipient** cancer.*

Insipid means dull, without flavor.
*The play's dialogue was **insipid**, so we left at intermission.*

Insipient means stupid or foolish.
*The article incisively pinpoints some of their **insipient** decisions.*

Incisive, Decided, Decisive

*See entry for **Decided, Decisive, Incisive**.*

Incite, Insight

Incite means to arouse or provoke action.
*Some political views tend to **incite** debate within a party.*

Insight refers to mental vision or understanding.
*Harold is offering his own **insights** on how to invest carefully.*

Inclose, Enclose

Enclose is preferred in American usage.
*Make sure you **enclose** your latest resume with the application.*

Incomparable, Incompatible

Incomparable means without equal.
*Apart from her **incomparable** beauty, she has a great voice.*

Incompatible means unable to get along or live together.
*Social Darwinism is **incompatible** with social facts.*

Incomprehensive, Incomprehensible, Uncomprehensible

Incomprehensive means incomplete, limited, or not extensive.
*The reviewers rejected the reference book as **incomprehensive**.*

Incomprehensible (or **uncomprehensible**) means cannot be understood.
*The writing was so poor it was practically **incomprehensible**.*

Inconceivable, Unthinkable

Inconceivable means incapable of being comprehended or explained.
*It's **inconceivable** that the merger will cost $30 billion.*

Unthinkable refers to something so undesirable or difficult to believe that it is unimaginable.
*It was once **unthinkable** for a man to go outside without a hat.*

Incredible, Incredulous

Incredible means hard to believe or unbelievable.
*Ed's quick explanation of the car accident is simply **incredible.***

Incredulous means not believing or skeptical.
*Rob's story of flying saucers received a few **incredulous** stares.*

Indeterminable, Indeterminate

Indeterminable means impossible to fix, measure, or decide.
*The impact on the number of applications is **indeterminable**.*

Indeterminate means vague or unclear.
*Objects with **indeterminate** boundaries are difficult to model.*

Indict, Indite

Indict means to accuse or formally charge.
*The grand jury is going to **indict** the suspect this week.*

Indite means to compose or put into writing.
*Our boss seldom uses a writer to help **indite** his speeches.*

Indictment, Arraignment

*See entry for **Arraignment, Indictment**.*

Indifferent, Ambiguous, Ambivalent

*See entry for **Ambiguous, Ambivalent, Indifferent**.*

Indigenous, Indigent, Indignant, Indignity

Indigenous means native.
***Indigenous** cultures can often contribute to medical discoveries.*

Indigent means in need of money, impoverished, or poor.
*The government provides medical care for **indigent** families.*

Indignant means angry.
*A full and detailed explanation backs Phil's **indignant** denial.*

Indignity refers to offending a person's dignity or self-respect.
*The hunger in the world is an **indignity** to mankind.*

Indiscreet, Indiscrete

Indiscreet means not showing prudent or good judgment.
*His open discussion of their financial problems was **indiscreet**.*

Indiscrete means not divided or divisible into separate parts.
*The soil consisted of **indiscrete** layers of sand, dirt, and gravel.*

Indolence, Insolence

Indolence means being lazy.
*A feeling of **indolence** usually overtakes them during vacation.*

Insolence means being cheeky, offensive, or conceited.
*The **insolence** from that immature student is not called for.*

Indubitable, Redoubtable, Undoubted

Indubitable means not open to question.
*It is **indubitable** that they were better prepared.*

Redoubtable means feared or worthy of respect.
*She is a **redoubtable** opponent; you must respect her.*

Undoubted means undisputed.
*For a player of his **undoubted** talent, he scores little.*

Inductive, Deductive

*See entry for **Deductive, Inductive**.*

Inedible, Uneatable, Unedible

Though today the preferred term is **inedible**, all three words are still considered synonyms.

Inequity, Iniquity

Inequity refers to injustice or unfairness.
*Many voters are unhappy about the **inequity** of the system.*

Iniquity refers to immorality, sin, or wickedness.
*The tribal sought to investigate the dictator's many **iniquities**.*

Inessential, Nonessential, Unessential

All three words are considered synonyms.

Inexpensive, Cheap

*See entry for **Cheap, Inexpensive**.*

Inexplicable, Inextricable

Inexplicable means difficult or impossible to explain.
*The TV show's **inexplicable** popularity pleases the sponsors.*

Inextricable means difficult or impossible to separate or avoid.
*The conflict is **inextricably** linked to poor communication.*

Infamous, Famous, Notorious

*See entry for **Famous, Infamous, Notorious**.*

Infectious, Contagious

*See entry for **Contagious, Infectious**.*

Infinity, Affinity, Eternity

*See entry for **Affinity, Eternity, Infinity**.*

Inflammable, Flammable, Nonflammable

*See entry for **Flammable, Inflammable, Nonflammable**.*

Inflict, Afflict

*See entry for **Afflict, Inflict**.*

Inform, Advise

*See entry for **Advise, Inform**.*

Informant, Informer

Informant is a person who gives information.
*We just learned that the **informant** was our neighbor.*

Informer is a person who is paid for information about others.
*The **informer** testified against Frank.*

Ingenious, Ingenuous, Disingenuous

*See entry for **Disingenuous, Ingenious, Ingenuous**.*

Ingress, Egress

Ingress refers to the legal right of the property owner *to enter* leased property. **Egress** refers to the legal right of a property owner *to leave* leased property.

Inhabitant, Habitant, Habitat

*See entry for **Habitant, Habitat, Inhabitant**.*

Inhuman, Inhumane

Inhuman means lacking human qualities like kindness or pity.
*It was **inhuman** of them to deprive him of time with his family.*

Inhumane means being cruel or insensitive to others.
*Many read about the **inhumane** treatment of the prisoners.*

Inimical, Inimitable

Inimical means harmful, hostile, or unfriendly.
*Their polices were **inimical** to democratic principles.*

Inimitable means defying imitation or matchless.
*The comedian entertained the audience in his **inimitable** way.*

Initialism, Abbreviation, Acronym

See entry for ***Abbreviation, Acronym, Initialism***.

Innervate, Enervate, Invigorate

See entry for ***Enervate, Innervate, Invigorate***.

Innumerable, Endless

See entry for ***Endless, Innumerable***.

Inquire, Enquire

Inquire is the preferred spelling, but either is acceptable.

Insidious, Invidious

Insidious means spreading harm in a subtle way.
*Her criticism has an **insidious** effect on the team's morale.*

Invidious means being discriminatory or causing resentment.
*The new laws appear to be unjust and **invidious** to many people.*

Insoluble, Insolvable, Insolvent

Insoluble means it cannot be dissolved.
*The high-protein soy powder is **insoluble** in milk.*

Insolvable means not easily solved.
*The corporation continues to have **insolvable** quality problems.*

Insolvent means incapable of paying debts.
*The owners are selling many assets of those **insolvent** companies.*

Install, Instill

Install means to put into position or to set up.
*Katie is going to **install** the new software after work.*

Instill means to implant or introduce gradually.
*The short preparation is not enough time to **instill** confidence.*

Instinct, Intuition

Instinct is an inborn tendency within an individual.
*A bear's **instinct** makes the animal hibernate in the winter.*

Intuition is knowledge of something without the use of reason.
*Brett's **intuition** told him to sell the stock before it crashed.*

Insure, Assure, Ensure

*See entry for **Assure, Ensure, Insure**.*

Intense, Intensive

Intense means occurring in an extreme degree or powerful.
*The heat last summer was so **intense**, several people died.*

Intensive means concentrated or thorough.
*The **intensive** care he got helped him recover from the accident.*

Intentionally, Advisedly

*See entry for **Advisedly, Intentionally**.*

Interment, Internment

Interment refers to a burial.
*The **interment** takes place soon after the religious service.*

Internment refers to confinement or imprisonment, without trial, of an enemy.
*The agency complained about the **internment** of the civilian.*

Intermittent, Occasional

Intermittent means starting and stopping at intervals.
***Intermittent** acute sun exposure can damage the skin.*

Occasional means infrequent or irregular.
*The **occasional** wash and wax won't keep my car looking good.*

Internet, Intranet

Internet, always capitalized, is a worldwide system of computer networks. **Intranet**, which doesn't need to be capitalized, is a much smaller and private network within an enterprise. The rarer term, *extranet*, can be viewed as a subset to a company's **intranet** that is extended to users outside the company.

Interpolate, Extrapolate

See entry for **Extrapolate, Interpolate***.*

Interpret, Interpretate

Interpretate is not a word.

Interpreter, Translator

An **interpreter** converts speech to another language, and a **translator** converts writing to another language.

Interstate, Intestate, Intrastate

Interstate means between states.
The 1956 Federal-Aid Highway Act brought America its **Interstate** *Highway System.*

Intestate means without a will.
The law of **intestate** *succession can vary from state to state.*

Intrastate means within one state.
The bill attempts to specifically regulate **intrastate** *commerce.*

Intolerable, Intolerant

Intolerable means tiring or unbearable.
He considered the store's poor service **intolerable***.*

Intolerant means biased, prejudiced, or unwilling to accept.
She was **intolerant** *of people who didn't see things her way.*

Introduction, Foreword, Preface

See entry for **Foreword, Introduction, Preface***.*

Introvert, Extrovert

Introvert refers to people who enjoy calm activities with few people. **Extrovert** refers to people who enjoy thrills with large groups of people.

Intrust, Entrust

*See entry for **Entrust, Intrust**.*

Inure, Enure

*See entry for **Enure, Inure**.*

Invaluable, Valueless

Invaluable means of great worth.
*Her talk gave us an **invaluable** insight into better living habits.*

Valueless means worth nothing.
*The jeweler told us our rings were almost **valueless**.*

Invent, Discover

*See entry for **Discover, Invent**.*

Invigorate, Enervate, Innervate

*See entry for **Enervate, Innervate, Invigorate**.*

Invoke, Evince, Evoke

*See entry for **Evince, Evoke, Invoke**.*

Inward, Inwards

Inward is preferred in American usage.

Irascible, Erasable

*See entry for **Erasable, Irascible**.*

Irregardless, Regardless

Irregardless is a nonstandard word. Avoid its use.

Regardless means without regard or unmindful.
*The foursome plays every Saturday **regardless** of the weather.*

Irrelevant, Irreverent

Irrelevant means not pertinent or not relating to the subject.
*Some of the testimony in the case seemed to be **irrelevant**.*

Irreverent means disrespectful, satirical, or lacking reverence.
*The Cub Scouts' **irreverent** behavior angered the scoutmaster.*

Irritate, Aggravate

See entry for **Aggravate, Irritate**.

Irruption, Eruption

See entry for **Eruption, Irruption**.

Isle, Aisle

See entry for **Aisle, Isle**.

Islet, Eyelet

Islet is a small island. **Eyelet** is small hole edged with embroidered stitches as part of a design.

Iterate, Reiterate

These words are synonyms that mean to repeat.

Its, It's

Its is a possessive pronoun that is never split by an apostrophe.
*Though outdated, our first computer has served **its** purpose.*

It's is the contracted or shortened form of *it is*.
***It's** definitely much faster than our first computer.*

Memory hook: Possessive *its* never *splits*.

Ivory tower, Ivy tower

Ivory tower, which refers to a remote place or an attitude of retreat, is the correct phrase. Originally inspired by the Bible's Song of Solomon, it was Henry James' 1916 novel of that title that embedded the phrase in the English vocabulary.
*What does he know about our situation, living as he does in an **ivory tower**?*

J

"The most valuable of all talents is that of never using two words when one will do."—Thomas Jefferson

Jail, Prison

A **jail** is a short-term detaining facility for those awaiting trial or for those convicted of minor offenses. A **prison**, sometimes referred to as a *penitentiary*, is a long-term detaining facility for those convicted of major offenses.

Jealous, Zealous

Jealous means intolerant of competition or suspicious of unfaithfulness.
*He was **jealous** about his co-worker's recent promotion.*
*Her husband shows signs of being **jealous** and insecure.*

Zealous means passionate or eager to pursue something.
*She was **zealous** in her pursuit of becoming a great musician.*

Jealousy, Envy

*See entry for **Envy, Jealousy**.*

Jell, Gel

*See entry for **Gel, Jell**.*

Jerry-built, Jury-built

Jerry-built, which carries a negative connotation, refers to a permanent, but poorly built, construction. The origin of the phrase is unclear, but it may have derived from the flimsy work of an English construction company called Jerry Brothers. **Jury-rigged**, which dates to the late 1700s nautical term *jury mast*, refers to a ship's temporary mast. It means something cleverly constructed in a makeshift manner for temporary use. Sometimes these two expressions are misstated as **jerry-rigged** or **jury-built**.

Jest, Gist
*See entry for **Gist, Jest**.*

Jester, Gesture
*See entry for **Gesture, Jester**.*

Jetsam, Flotsam
*See entry for **Flotsam, Jetsam**.*

Jibe, Gibe
*See entry for **Gibe, Jibe**.*

Judgement, Judgment
Judgment without the first e is preferred in American usage.
*We reserve **judgment** until all the facts are available.*

Judicial, Judicious, Juridical
Judicial refers to the law courts or judges.
*The **judicial** branch is just one branch of the U.S. Government.*

Judicious refers to a person's careful or wise judgment.
*The taxpayers want to see **judicious** spending.*

Juridical refers to the administration of justice.
*He proceeded to fulfill the **juridical** requirements of the case.*

Jump start, Kick start
Jump start refers to getting something started or revived such as a weak economy. **Kick start** refers to starting a motorcycle.

Junction, Juncture
These words are usually used interchangeably.

Jurist, Juror
A **jurist** is an expert in law (a judge or legal scholar), and a **juror** is a member of the jury.

K

"Words are, of course, the most powerful drug used by mankind."—
Rudyard Kipling

Kamikaze, Hara-kiri

Kamikaze is Japanese suicide by crashing an aircraft on the enemy, and **Hara-kiri** is Japanese suicide by slitting the belly.

Karat, Carat, Caret, Carrot

*See entry for **Carat, Caret, Carrot, Karat.***

Kick start, Jump start

Kick start refers to starting a motorcycle. **Jump start** refers to getting something started or revived such as a weak economy.

Kind of, Sort of

Avoid these awkward phrases if you mean ***somewhat***.
*The concert was **somewhat** (not **kind of** or **sort of**) boring.*

Kin, Kith

Kin refers to family or relatives. **Kith** refers to acquaintances, friends, or neighbors.

Know-how

Avoid this colloquial and informal phrase in formal writing.
*They have a reputation for exceptional knowledge (not **know-how**) on this topic.*

Koala bear

A **koala** is a marsupial *not* a bear. Just call these animals **koalas**.

L

"So difficult is it to show the various meanings and imperfections of words when we have nothing else but words to do it with."
—John Locke

Lager, Ale

Both beverages are beer types. **Ale** is produced with a top-fermenting yeast, fermenting between 64 and 70 degrees. **Lager** is produced with a bottom-fermenting yeast, fermenting between 52 and 58 degrees. The difference in temperature can affect the taste. **Ales** typically are fruitier and **lagers** more crisp.

Landslide, Avalanche

A **landslide** is an entire mountainside coming down. An **avalanche** refers to snow, rocks, or other debris coming down a mountainside.

Languid, Limp, Limpid

Languid means lacking energy or vitality.
With languid waves of the hand, they said their goodbyes.

Limp, as an adjective, means lacking in stiffness.
The limp lettuce ruined the chef's salad.

Limpid means crystal clear.
Limpid streams are found in this mountainous area.

Lapse, Elapse

See entry for Elapse, Lapse.

Latin Abbreviations

Here are some common Latin abbreviations and their meanings:

e.g. (exempli gratia) means *for example.*
etc. (et cetera) means *and other things.*
ibid. (ibidem) means *in the same place.*
i.e. (id est) means *that is* or *that is to say.*

Latter, Former

Former refers to the first of two and **latter** the second of two (or last of many). Note that when you use these words, the reader must remember what was written. This can sometimes be annoying, so you might want to reconsider using these words.

Laudable, Laudatory

Laudable means worthy of praise.
*The celebrity returned home for a **laudable** cause.*

Laudatory means expressing praise.
*The concert last night received a **laudatory** review.*

Lawful, Legal

Lawful means rightful or in accordance with the law.
*The elder son is the **lawful** heir to much of the estate.*
*He transferred the ownership of the property in a **lawful** way.*

Legal means relating to the law.
*The **legal** arena is addressing the downloading of various media.*

Lawyer, Attorney

In everyday usage and American English, the terms are synonyms; however, per some dictionaries, a **lawyer** can provide legal advice and has been trained all about laws. An **attorney** is *legally permitted* to represent people or act in their behalf.

Note: Some attorneys and lawyers use just the word *Esquire* before their names.

Lay, Lie

Lay means to place or to put something; it requires a direct object.
*Where are you going to **lay** that book?*
*I am **laying** the book on the kitchen counter.*
*He **laid** the book on the kitchen counter.*

Lie means to be in a horizontal position; it never takes an object.
*The baseball **lies** in the street next to the car.*
*The baseball is **lying** by the car.*
*How long has the baseball **lain** in the street?*

Leach, Leech

Leach, a verb, means to empty, drain, or remove.
*The contaminated water **leached** into the neighborhood soil.*

Leech, a noun, refers to a bloodsucking worm or a person who will pillage from another.
***Leeches** are usually found in cool fresh water, rivers, and ponds.*
*We discovered a few people **leeching** off our wireless Internet.*

Leaflet, Brochure, Pamphlet

*See entry for **Brochure, Leaflet, Pamphlet**.*

*The chicken **lays** an egg while the farmer **lies** in the hay.*

Leak, Leek

Leak refers to the escape or passage of something.
*All of the water **leaked** out of his canteen while he was hiking.*

Leek refers to an edible plant (part of the onion family).
*Rick grew beets, tomatoes, and **leeks** in his garden.*

Lean, Lien

Lean, as an adjective, means having a low fat content. As a verb, it means to incline.
*Venison is **lean** compared with many meats we have eaten.*
*Do not **lean** against the door of the train.*

Lien means a legal claim to something.
*The bank has a **lien** against their vacation home in New Jersey.*

Learn, Teach

Learn means to acquire information or knowledge.
*This computer game helps people **learn** how to read.*

Teach means to impart knowledge or information.
*Some English teachers still **teach** how to diagram sentences.*

Leastways, At least

*See entry for **At least, Leastways**.*

Leave, Let

Leave means to allow to remain or to go away.
*If you **leave** the book with me, I'll be sure to read it.*
*If you **leave** quietly, no one in the library will be disturbed.*

Let means to allow or to permit.
*Please **let** me help you with your chemistry homework.*

Note: When **leave** or **let** is used with the word *alone*, these words are interchangeable.
***Leave (let)** Gerry alone while he is doing his homework.*

Lectern, Podium, Pulpit, Rostrum

Lectern is a small slanted stand that supports papers or books.
Podium is an elevated small platform where one stands. A **pulpit**
is the same as a lectern but found in a church. **Rostrum** is also a
platform but larger than a **podium** and usually more decorative.

Memory hook: You stand *behind* a **lectern** or **pulpit** and *on* a
podium or **rostrum**.

Legation, Ligation

Legation refers to the premises occupied by a diplomatic minister
and staff.
*The French **legation** is the residence of the chargé d'affaires.*

Ligation refers to binding or applying a ligature (as in surgery).
***Ligation** and stripping is a surgery used on varicose veins.*

Legend, Fable, Myth, Parable

*See entry for **Fable, Legend, Myth, Parable**.*

Legislator, Legislature

Legislator refers to a lawmaker.
*The **legislator** proposed a law that limits tobacco sales.*

Legislature refers to a group of lawmakers.
*The election brought 10 new members to the city **legislature**.*

Lend, Loan

Lend is a verb.
*Please **lend** me $20.*

Loan is a noun.
*The $20 is a gift not a **loan**.*

Note: Although careful writers maintain this distinction, it is
common to see **lend** and **loan** used interchangeably as verbs.

Less, Fewer, Lest

*See entry for **Fewer, Less, Lest**.*

Lessee, Lessor

Lessee refers to a lease holder or tenant.
*The **lessee** makes the rental payments on the 15th of every month.*

Lessor refers to a lease grantor or landlord.
*The **lessor** keeps full ownership rights of the apartment.*

Lessen, Lesson

Lessen means to diminish or become less.
*My broker says bond funds may **lessen** investment risk.*

Lesson is something to be learned.
*The new software helps teachers make detailed **lesson** plans.*

Levee, Levy

Levee is a formal reception or an embankment.
*The new consul was introduced at a **levee** near the embassy.*
*After the **levee** broke, the town quickly evacuated.*

Levy, a verb, means to impose, enlist, or begin war.
*The court could **levy** a fine for misappropriating the funds.*
*They are going to **levy** troops from the countryside.*
*They want to avoid **levying** war at all costs.*

Levy, a noun, is a charge imposed or the act of levying money, property, or troops.
*The tax rate **levy** is a real challenge this year.*
*The recent **levy** raised few troops for the military.*

Liable, Libel, Lible, Slander

Liable means legally responsible or likely.
*The jury quickly found him **liable** for fraud.*
*Considering the dark clouds, it is **liable** to rain today.*

Libel is damaging someone's reputation in print or other media.
*The inaccurate story prompted him to sue for **libel**.*

Lible is not a word.

Slander is an oral statement that damages a person's reputation.
*His negative comments toward him were taken as **slander**.*

Ligament, Tendon

A **ligament** is the strong connective tissue that connects bones or cartilage at a joint. A **tendon** is the fibrous tissue that connects the muscle to the bone.

Lightening, Lightning

Lightening means making lighter.
*John can never be accused of **lightening** the workload.*

Lightning is an atmospheric electrical charge.
*If you are not careful, golf clubs can act like **lightning** rods.*

Like, As

*See entry for **As, Like**.*

Like how, Like in, Like when

Avoid these phrases because **like** is a preposition and should be followed by a noun, noun phrase, or pronoun.
*They dressed **as** (not **like how**) they did in the 1970s.*
*They dressed **like** (not **like in**) disco dancers from the 1970s.*
*Jim does things for the poor, **like** (not **like when**) serving free meals.*

Likely, Apt

*See entry for **Apt, Likely**.*

Limit, Limitation

Limit refers to a physical or political boundary.
*They say there may be no **limit** to how long people can live.*

Limitation refers to a restraint or restriction.
*Some states have a **limitation** on cell phone use in cars.*

Linage, Lineage

Linage refers to the number of lines of printed material.
*The newspaper charges its advertisers by ad size and **linage**.*

Lineage refers to ancestry, line of descent, or derivation.
*The family could trace their **lineage** to the 14th century.*

Liqueur, Liquor

A **liqueur** (or cordial) is a sweet, strong, highly flavored alcoholic drink. **Liquor** is an alcoholic beverage (such as whiskey) made by distillation rather than by fermentation (such as wine or beer). **Liquor** is also a broth derived by cooking meats or vegetables for a long time.

Listen, Hear

*See entry for **Hear, Listen**.*

Litany, Liturgy

Litany refers to a form of prayer or a lengthy list.
*The **Litany** of the Saints is read at our church every Sunday.*
*The accused faced a **litany** of questions about his whereabouts.*

Liturgy refers to the prescribed form for a religious service.
*Today's worship service is built around the **liturgy** of celebration.*

Literally, Literately, Figuratively

*See entry for **Figuratively, Literally, Literately**.*

Lo and behold, Low and behold

Lo and behold is the correct phrase.

Load, Lode

Load refers to a quantity of something that can be carried at one time. **Lode** refers to an ore deposit, usually a large amount.

Loath, Loathe

Loath means reluctant or unwilling.
*Henry is **loath** to move despite the attractive job offer.*

Loathe means to dislike intensely.
*Every month we **loathe** receiving those credit card bills.*

Locale, Locality, Location

Locale is a place associated with a particular event or occurrence.
*The film producers found a **locale** in Mexico for the sequel.*

Locality is a particular neighborhood, place, or district.
*Our vacation house is in a quiet **locality** not far from the shore.*

Location is a place where something is situated.
*The **location** of the damaged part has not been determined.*

Loch, Lock

Loch is a lake (e.g., *Loch Nest monster*). **Lock** can be a door fastening for security or a canal gated at each end that raises or lowers watercraft from one level to another (*the locks of St. Lawrence River*).

Loop, Loupe

Loop refers to a circle of something.
*Take that **loop** around the city to avoid the traffic backup.*

Loupe is a jeweler's magnifying tool held near the eye.
*We looked at the diamond through a **loupe** and saw flaws.*

Loose, Lose

Loose means unrestrained or not tight.
*Giant icebergs continue to shake **loose** off the Antarctic coast.*

Lose means to mislay or miss out on something.
*By not accepting credit cards, companies can **lose** potential sales.*

Loosen, Unloosen

Loosen is the correct word. The *un* is not needed.

Lux, Luxe

Lux is a physics term for a unit of measurement of illumination.
*The object was almost three **lux** from the original light source.*

Luxe refers to something elegant or luxurious.
*Our hotel room was quite **luxe** and spacious.*

Luxuriant, Luxurious

Luxuriant refers to something abundant, profuse, or rich.
Luxuriant lawns and gardens surround the hotel on all sides.

Luxurious refers to luxury.
*The vacation package includes a weekend stay at a **luxurious** hotel.*

M

"I love writing. I love the swirl and swing of words as they tangle with human emotions."—James A. Michener

Macrocosm, Microcosm

Macrocosm is any large, complex entity and **microcosm** is a miniature representation of something.

Magnate, Magnet

Magnate is a powerful person (usually in business).
*The shipping **magnate** donates money to cancer research.*

Magnet is a person or thing that exerts attraction.
*The low cost of living there is a **magnet** for the retired.*

Magnificent, Magniloquent, Munificent

Magnificent means grand or splendid.
*The Hearst Castle has a **magnificent** view of the ocean.*

Magniloquent means colorful, extravagant, or lofty in speech.
*My professor's **magniloquent** talks are entertaining but confusing.*

Munificent means extremely generous.
*The celebrities gave a **munificent** donation to the relief effort.*

Majority, Plurality

Majority means more than 50 percent.
*The **majority** of the country favored last year's tax cut.*

Plurality means the most of something, even if it is less than 50 percent.
*Clinton won the Presidency with a **plurality** of the votes.*

Malevolence, Benevolence

*See entry for **Benevolence, Malevolence**.*

Malignant, Benign

Malignant means life threatening, and **benign** means not dangerous.

Maniac, Manic

Maniac is a crazy person, and **manic** is a clinical term referring to mania, excitement, or some psychological affliction (*manic depression*).

Manner, Manor

A **manner** is a way of acting or the way in which something is done. *His **manner** of speaking and delivery is quite articulate.*

A **manor** is a mansion or the principal residence on an estate. *The village's houses range from **manor** houses to quaint cottages.*

*The shipping **magnate** plays with his favorite **magnet**.*

Mantel, Mantle

A **mantel** is a shelf (mantelpiece).
*The couple placed a prized piece of art over their **mantel**.*

A **mantle** is a cloak or something that covers like a cloak.
*This morning a **mantle** of fog hung over the valley for hours.*

Many, Much

Many refers to countable items or units.
***Many** students volunteered their time for the charity.*

Much refers to noncountable items or units.
*Low-octane fuel caused **much** of our car trouble.*

Marital, Martial

Marital refers to marriage.
*The couple tried to resolve their **marital** difficulties.*

Martial refers to battle, military life, or war.
*The president declared **martial** law.*

Marked, Remarkable

Marked means clearly defined and evident.
*We noticed that Jack has a **marked** limp when he walks.*

Remarkable means extraordinary or worthy of notice.
*We noticed a **remarkable** improvement in Gerry's grades.*

Masseur, Masseuse

Masseur is a male massage therapist, and **masseuse** is a female massage therapist.

Masterful, Masterly

Masterful means domineering or powerful.
*General George Patton was a **masterful** soldier and leader.*

Masterly means highly skilled.
*His spring concert was a **masterly** performance of Bach.*

Material, Materiel

Material is the substance from which something is composed.
*His new suit is made of a light blue silk **material**.*

Materiel is the equipment or supplies used by an organization.
*The convoy brought **materiel** to the base.*

May, Can, Could, Might

*See entry for **Can, Could, May, Might**.*

May be, Maybe

May be is a verb phrase indicating possibility.
*On this matter, it **may be** necessary to ask for a second opinion.*

Maybe is an adverb meaning *perhaps*.
***Maybe** the legal staff can resolve this issue within a few days.*

May have, May of

May have is the correct phrase.
*As you **may have** heard by now, tonight's class was cancelled.*

Mayoral, Mayoralty

Mayoral (an adjective) refers to matters concerning the officer
(mayor) or the office.
*The **mayoral** election is in June, and it's already contentious.*

Mayoralty (a noun) refers to the office or term of a mayor.
*Mr. Daily was well suited for the **mayoralty**.*

Mean, Median

Mean is the sum of all numbers in a group divided by the
number of figures. It is commonly called the *average*.
*The arithmetic **mean** of 1, 5, and 6 is $(1 + 5 + 6) \div 3 = 4$.*

Median is the midpoint of a range of numbers. To find a median,
write the numbers in order from largest to smallest. The figure
with the same number of figures above and below is the median.
*The **median** of 12, 19, 23, 45, and 60 is 23.*

Mean, Mien

Mean, an adjective, means lacking kindness.
*Though the dog looks **mean,** he is just a playful puppy.*

Mien, a noun, refers to a person's manner or appearance.
*Annie is known for her noble **mien**, virtue, and great appeal.*

Meantime, Meanwhile

Both words refer to an intervening time.

Meantime is commonly used as a noun.
*In the **meantime**, we continue to wait for another opportunity.*

Meanwhile is commonly used as an adverb.
***Meanwhile**, we waited an extra hour for the children to arrive.*

Meddle, Mettle

Meddle means to interfere with something.
*We have no desire to **meddle** in the politics of our community.*

Mettle refers to the quality or strength of a person's character.
*Rachel is being given a chance to prove her **mettle** and worth.*

Media are, Media is

Media are is correct because **media** is the plural of *medium*.
*All the news **media are** covering the events of the trial.*

Mediate, Arbitrate, Adjudicate

*See entry for **Adjudicate, Arbitrate, Mediate**.*

Melody, Tune

A **melody** is a group of notes in a certain order that results in a nice sound. A **tune** is an easily remembered *melody*.

Memento, Momento

Memento is a special remembrance or souvenir.
*Joe brought back a **memento** from England for his wife.*

Note: In Catholicism, **memento** refers to the Canon of the Mass. **Momento** is not a word.

Mendacity, Mendicity

Mendacity refers to lying or dishonesty.
*An odor of **mendacity** hung over his testimony at the hearing.*

Mendicity means begging.
*This law curbs behavior such as **mendicity**.*

Meretricious, Meritorious

Meretricious means fake, flashy, or attractive in a bad way.
*Though sharp, his arguments were deemed **meretricious**.*

Meritorious means deserving of praise, reward, and honor.
*The mayor recognized Jan for **meritorious** service to the town.*

Metaphor, Simile

Metaphor and **simile** are comparisons that are quite different, but are commonly confused simply because they are so similar. A **metaphor** is a definitive comparison that does not use the words *like* or *as*. (*A wire is a road for electrons*.) A **simile** is an approximation that uses the words *like* or *as*. (*A good book is like a good meal*.)

Meteor, Asteroid, Meteorite, Meteoroid

*See entry for **Asteroid, Meteor, Meteorite, Meteoroid**.*

Meteorology, Metrology

Meteorology is the science of weather. **Metrology** is the science of measurement.

Method, Methodology

Method is a way to do something.
*What **method** did the golf pro use to fix Bill's slice?*

Methodology is a set of methods, procedures, or rules.
*He introduced a different **methodology** of linguistics.*

Meticulous, Scrupulous

Meticulous means exact, finicky, or precise.
*The Saratoga artist shows a **meticulous** attention to detail.*

Scrupulous means conscientious or principled.
*A **scrupulous** character tries to stay within the letter of the law.*

Midget, Dwarf

A **midget** is a very short person with proportioned body parts, and a **dwarf** is a very short person with disproportionate body parts. Because these two words have fallen out of favor, prefer the terms *short person* or *little person.*

Might have, Might of

Might have is the correct phrase.
*Do you think they **might have** gone without him?*

Migrant, Emigrant, Immigrant

*See entry for **Emigrant, Immigrant, Migrant**.*

Militate, Mitigate

Militate means to influence or oppose something.
*The leader's anger **militated** against any hope of a truce.*

Mitigate means to diminish in severity or to lessen.
*The physical therapy for my neck **mitigated** the severe pain.*

Milk toast, Milquetoast

Milk toast refers to buttered toast usually served in warm milk with sugar and seasonings. **Milquetoast** refers to a shy, timid, or unassertive person. The origin of the word is a cartoon character, Caspar Milquetoast, who starred in Harold Webster's comic strip *The Timid Soul* (1924 to 1953).

Millenary, Millinery

Millenary refers to a 1,000. **Millinery** refers to women's hats.

Millennium, Century

A **millennium** is 1,000 years, and a **century** is 100 years.

Minimize, Diminish

*See entry for **Diminish, Minimize**.*

Minion, Minyan

Minion is a subordinate, servant, follower, or dependent. **Minyan** is a quorum, the number of adult Jewish men required for a communal religious service.

Miniscule, Minuscule

Minuscule is the preferred spelling.
*The thorough study shows the disadvantages are **minuscule**.*

Mishap, Accident, Incident

*See entry for **Accident, Incident, Mishap**.*

Misinformation, Disinformation

*See entry for **Disinformation, Misinformation**.*

Misplace, Displace

*See entry for **Displace, Misplace**.*

Misuse, Abuse

*See entry for **Abuse, Misuse**.*

Mobile, Movable

Mobile means it can move, and **movable** means it can be moved.

Monetary, Fiscal

Monetary applies to money supply, and **fiscal** applies to budgetary matters.

Monogamy, Bigamy, Polygamy

*See entry for **Bigamy, Monogamy, Polygamy**.*

Moot point, Mute point

Moot point, a legal term dating to the mid 16th century, is the correct phrase. Then it specifically referred to hypothetical cases debated by law students. Because these debates were hypothetical, the phrase's meaning eventually changed to *not worth debating* or *of little significance*.

Moral, Morale

Moral as an adjective, means righteous. As a noun, a **moral** is a principle.
*They continually show a **moral** dimension to their actions.*
*What **moral** or message can be drawn from today's reading?*

Morale refers to the spirit or state of mind.
*Despite the surprise loss, we maintain a high team **morale**.*

More important, More importantly

Prefer **more important** because the *ly* is unnecessary. (**Important** is an adjective and modifies a noun, and **importantly** is an adverb and modifies a verb.)
***More important**, we make education a fun experience (correct).*
***More importantly**, we make education a fun experience (incorrect).*

Note: The same guideline applies to the phrase *most importantly*.

More so, Moreso

Despite the frequent use of **moreso**, it is not a word. Always spell it as two words (**more so**).

More than, Over

More than refers to countable items.
***More than** 500 churches are in upstate New York.*

Over refers to general amounts or unspecified increments.
***Over** half of the inventory is unsold, resulting in a huge loss.*

Most, Almost

*See entry for **Almost, Most**.*

Mother-in-laws, Mothers-in-law

Mothers-in-law is the correct phrase.

Motif, Motive

Motif is a main idea, element, or central theme in a work of art.
*A musical **motif** in Carmen occurs in the fortune-telling scene.*

Motive means incentive or goal or object of one's actions.
*What was your **motive** in confronting the sales manager?*

Motto, Slogan

A **motto** is a short phrase that usually expresses a moral aim or purpose. A **slogan** is a catch phrase used by a political party, fraternity, or other organization in advertising or promotion.

Much, Muchly

Muchly is not a word.
*We would **much** (not **muchly**) appreciate your attendance.*

Mucus, Mucous

Mucus is the noun and **mucous** is the adjective.
***Mucus** is emanating from the **mucous** glands.*

Multilateral, Bilateral, Unilateral

*See entry for **Bilateral, Multilateral, Unilateral**.*

Munitions, Ammunition

*See entry for **Ammunition, Munitions**.*

Must have, Must of

Must have is the correct phrase.
*The bank **must have** seen that foreclosure coming for weeks.*

Mutant, Mutation

A **mutant** refers to an organism arising from a **mutation**. A **mutation** is a new physical characteristic arising from a genetic anomaly.

Mutual, Common, Ordinary, Popular

*See entry for **Common, Mutual, Ordinary, Popular**.*

Mysterious, Mystical

Mysterious means beyond human comprehension or unintelligible.
*A **mysterious** craft appeared in the sky and left us wondering.*

Mystical means hidden from human knowledge (spiritual).
*The Blessed Mother's apparition at Fatima was a **mystical** experience.*

Myth, Fable, Legend, Parable

See entry for Fable, Legend, Myth, Parable.

N

"Those for whom words have lost their value are likely to find that ideas have also lost their value."—Edwin Newman

Nadir, Zenith

Nadir (lowest point) is the point on the celestial sphere directly below the observer, exactly opposite the **zenith** (highest point).
*They reached a **nadir** of despair when they lost their home.*
*When we adopted our son, we reached the **zenith** in our lives.*

Nascent, Nescient

Nascent means coming into existence or emerging.
*The **nascent** economic recovery appeared to stall.*

Nescient means lacking knowledge, ignorant, or nonbeliever.
*Their **nescient** level of the matter was surprising.*

Nation, Country

A **nation** is a body of people associated with a particular area or territory. A **country** is a piece of land or area and the home of certain people.

Naturalist, Naturist

A **naturalist** is someone interested in natural history, especially botany or zoology. A **naturist** is a person who practices nudity for reasons of health or religion.

Nauseated, Nauseous

Nauseated means to feel sick.
*Joe feels **nauseated** 20 minutes after his workout.*

Nauseous is an adjective meaning sickening.
*The neighbors refuse to put up with that **nauseous** stench.*

Naval, Navel

Naval refers to a navy.
*Many **naval** vessels are anchored in the harbor.*

Navel refers to the belly button or the *navel* orange.
*The doctor clamped the cord next to the baby's **navel**.*
*The **navel** orange is among the most popular of all oranges.*

Neither, Either

*See entry for **Either, Neither**.*

Nibble, Nybble

Nibble refers to a quick, small bite or morsel of food. **Nybble** refers to four bits in computer terminology.

Nip it in the bud, Nip it in the butt

Nip it in the bud, meaning to stop something while it is still in development, is the correct expression. This phrase refers to the de-budding of plants, allowing the remaining buds to grow better.
*The boss wants to **nip** that questionable practice **in the bud**.*

No body, Nobody

No body means no group.
***No body** of rules enacted by them can be called perfect.*

Nobody means no person.
*Star Trek went where **nobody** had gone before.*

No one

Always spell this as two words.
***No one** picks up the mail while we are away.*

No sooner than, No sooner when

No sooner than is correct. In this phrase, the word **sooner** is a comparative adverb and should be followed by **than** (not **when**).
*We had **no sooner** left the game **than** a batter hit a home run.*

177

Nohow

Nohow, nonstandard for *in no way* or *not at all*. Try to avoid.
*The clerk could **in no way** (not **nohow**) decipher the handwriting.*

Noisome, Noisy

Noisome means foul-smelling, noxious, or offensive.
*The **noisome** odor coming from the river bothers the residents.*

Noisy means making much noise.
*Despite the PC's high price, the keyboard is quite **noisy**.*

*The **noisome** odor drifted into the **noisy** party.*

Nonessential, Inessential, Unessential
All three of these words are considered synonyms.

Nonflammable, Flammable, Inflammable
See entry for *Flammable, Inflammable, Nonflammable*.

Northward, Northwards
Northward is preferred in American usage.

Notable, Noticeable
Notable means worthy of notice.
*Her accomplishments in chemistry are **notable**.*

Noticeable means readily observed.
*The construction crew is making **noticeable** progress.*

Nothing like
Avoid this awkward phrase and prefer the phrase **not nearly**.
*The crowd today is **not nearly** as loud as yesterday.*

Notorious, Famous, Infamous
See entry for *Famous, Infamous, Notorious*.

Novice, Amateur
See entry for *Amateur, Novice*.

Nowhere, Nowheres
Always use **nowhere**.

Nowhere near
Nowhere near is colloquial and should be avoided in writing. Use *not nearly* or *does not approach* instead.
*Vitamin water is **not nearly** as good for you as you think.*

Number, Amount
See entry for *Amount, Number*.

Numerable, Numerous

Numerable refers to something that can be counted or numbered.
*If the data are not **numerable**, the impact cannot be measured.*

Numerous means a great number of or many.
*The election officials tried saving **numerous** flawed ballots.*

Nutritional, Nutritious

Nutritional means related to the nutrition process (using food to support life).
*This chart contains **nutritional** information for certain menu items.*

Nutritious means healthy to eat or nourishing.
*To increase energy, eat **nutritious** foods like eggs, fruit, or whole grain breads.*

O

"Language ought to be the joint creation of poets and manual workers."—George Orwell

Oblivious, Obvious

Oblivious means unaware or unmindful of something.
*He was **oblivious** to the danger of the sun's ultra violet rays.*

Obvious means easily perceived or understood.
*Our services present **obvious** benefits to your company.*

Oblivious, Forgetful

*See entry for **Forgetful, Oblivious**.*

Observance, Observation

Observance refers to the following of a custom, duty, or law.
*The **observance** of Veterans Day varies throughout the state.*

Observation refers to the act of noticing or recording.
*The technician made careful **observations** during the test.*

Obsolescent, Obsolete

Obsolescent is the process of passing out of use or usefulness.
*Although turntables are **obsolescent**, they continue to sell well.*

Obsolete means no longer in use (outmoded in design, style, or construction).
*The Senate is considering a bill to close **obsolete** military bases.*

Obtain, Attain

*See entry for **Attain, Obtain**.*

Obtuse, Abstruse

*See entry for **Abstruse, Obtuse**.*

Occasional, Intermittent
*See entry for **Intermittent, Occasional**.*

Occultist, Oculist
Occultist is one who believes in or studies supernatural things.
*An **occultist** would usually reject astronomy in favor of astrology.*

Oculist is a physician who treats eyes (synonymous with
ophthalmologist and optometrist).
***Oculist** Dr. Smith treated my glaucoma.*

Octave, Scale
Octave is the distance covered by any eight notes of a scale. A
scale is a series of eight notes played in alphabetical order.

*The coach was **oblivious** to his star batter's **obvious** bad habits.*

Odious, Odoriferous, Odorous

Odious means distasteful or offensive.
*Jane thinks cleaning the oven is an **odious** task.*

Odoriferous means having an odor or fragrance.
*Perfume is a blend of certain **odoriferous** substances.*

Odorous refers to something smelly.
*The **odorous** materials need to be placed in plastic bags.*

Odor, Aroma

Odor refers to an unpleasant smell (*a kitchen's foul odor*), and
aroma refers to a pleasing smell (*cake's aroma*).

Of, Have

*See entry for **Have, Of**.*

Official, Officious

Official, as an adjective, means authorized or formal. As a noun,
it means a person who holds an office.
*Here is an **official** announcement: schools will be closed Friday.*
*The **official** always makes the final ruling.*

Officious means meddling in other people's affairs.
*They opposed any **officious** interference with personal matters.*

Often, Oftentimes

Often is the preferred and simpler word to use.
***Often** (not **oftentimes**) we exercise immediately after work.*

OK, Okay

Avoid these expressions in *formal* writing.
*We gave our approval (not **OK** or **okay**) to the new project.*

Old-fashion, Old-fashioned

Old-fashioned, meaning outdated, is the correct phrase to use.
*Bob uses an **old-fashioned** approach for teaching applied math.*

Omnipotent, Omnipresent, Omniscient

Omnipotent means all powerful or unlimited authority.
*According to most religious people, God is **omnipotent**.*

Omnipresent means to be present everywhere simultaneously.
*Technological change is **omnipresent** throughout the world.*

Omniscient means to be all knowing or have total knowledge.
*If he were **omniscient**, he would know how Jenny feels.*

Omnivorous, Carnivorous, Herbivorous

*See entry for **Carnivorous, Herbivorous, Omnivorous**.*

On route, En route

En route, meaning on the way, is the correct phrase.
*We were told the package is **en route** from the factory.*

On tenderhooks, On tenterhooks

On tenterhooks, meaning to be as tense as the canvas being stretched into a tent, is the correct phrase.

On to, Onto

On to is used when **on** is an adverb and **to** is a preposition.
*The engineers then moved **on to** the next phase of the project.*

Onto means to move to a position or to be aware of something.
*You can transfer pictures **onto** your computer in a few steps.*
*We are **onto** your plan for restructuring the company.*

One and the same, One in the same

One and the same is the correct phrase.

One another, Each other

*See entry for **Each other, One another**.*

One of the best, One of the only

Avoid these contradictions. (There can only be one *best* and one *only*, so saying *one of the best* or *only* doesn't make sense.)

Oral

Onward, Onwards
Onward is preferred in American usage.

Opaque, Translucent, Transparent
Opaque means no light passing through.
*The **opaque** camera cover protected the film.*

Translucent means light passes through but without clarity.
***Translucent** bond paper is often used for tracing.*

Transparent means light passes through with clarity.
*The **transparent** lid allowed Mom to see the leftovers inside.*

Ophthalmologist, Optician, Optometrist
An **ophthalmologist** is an M.D. who specializes in treating eye diseases. An **optician** makes and sells glasses and other optical equipment. An **optometrist** examines one's vision and prescribes eye glasses.

Oppose, Appose
*See entry for **Appose, Oppose**.*

Opposite, Apposite
*See entry for **Apposite, Opposite**.*

Oppress, Repress
Oppress means to tyrannize or treat people in a cruel way.
*Their goal is to **oppress** the people of other countries.*

Repress means to restrain, subdue, or keep under control.
*Never try not to **repress** your feelings of joy and happiness.*

Oral, Aural
*See entry for **Aural, Oral**.*

Oral, Verbal
Oral and **verbal** both refer to things spoken; **verbal** also refers to things written.
*Graduate students are required to do an **oral** report this year.*
*Writer Albert M. Joseph has a **verbal** mastery of our language.*

Ordinal numbers, Cardinal numbers

*See entry for **Cardinal numbers, Ordinal numbers**.*

Ordinance, Ordnance

Ordinance refers to a decree, law, or regulation.
*Commissioners are discussing an **ordinance** to improve the park.*

Ordnance refers to military equipment or weapons.
*The technology can help find unexploded **ordnance**.*

Ordinary, Common, Mutual, Popular

*See entry for **Common, Mutual, Ordinary, Popular**.*

*Jim got a citation for breaking the local **ordinance**
against keeping **ordnance** in a residence.*

Orient, Orientate

Orient is the preferred word.
*We have plenty of time to **orient** ourselves to the project.*

Orthoscopic, Arthroscopic

Arthroscopic is the correct word.
*The surgeon performed **arthroscopic** surgery on his left knee.*

Oscillate, Osculate

Oscillate means to swing back and forth or to be indecisive.
*The speed **oscillated** between 280 rpm and 600 rpm.*
*His political career **oscillated** between distinction and scandal.*

Osculate means to kiss or to touch.
*His chief political skill was **osculating** the infants of voters.*

Ostensibly, Ostentatiously

Ostensibly means apparently, evidently, or presumably.
*It's a story **ostensibly** for kids, but more appreciated by adults.*

Ostentatiously is an adverb meaning showy or pretentious.
*They rarely dress **ostentatiously** and never flaunt their wealth.*

Ought to, Had ought to

Had ought to is incorrect. Just the phrase **ought to** is sufficient.
*He **ought to** have gone to the party instead of staying home.*

Out loud, Aloud

*See entry for **Aloud, Out loud**.*

Outmost, Upmost, Utmost

Outmost means outermost or farthest out.
*Jan made a trip to the **outmost** reaches of northern Alaska.*

Upmost is from the word *uppermost* and should not be used in American English.

Utmost usually means to the greatest degree or intensity.
*Our department treats all matters with **utmost** confidentiality.*

Outward, Outwards

Outward is preferred in American usage.

Over, More than

*See entry for **More than, Over**.*

Overdo, Overdue

Overdo means to do in excess.
*I'll try not to **overdo** the caffeine, which is my weakness.*

Overdue refers to the past time when something is due.
*His rent was **overdue** by three months.*

Overexaggerate, Exaggerate

Overexaggerate is not a word. **Exaggerate** alone is sufficient.

Overlook, Oversee

Overlook means to fail to notice, to disregard, or to ignore.
*We **overlooked** the fact that he failed to win the big game.*

Oversee means to direct, supervise, or manage.
*He was hired to **oversee** the manufacturing site.*

Overt, Covert

*See entry for **Covert, Overt**.*

Overweening, Overwhelming

Overweening means conceited, overbearing, or pretentious.
*We feel his **overweening** ego would not fit with the rest of us.*

Overwhelming means overpowering in effect or strength.
*Doctors feel the artificial heart is an **overwhelming** success.*

P

"A good word makes the heart glad."—Proverbs

Palate, Palette, Pallet

Palate is the roof of your mouth.
*A cleft **palate** is a common birth defect.*

Palette is a hand-held board that an artist uses for mixing paint.
*His **palette** contains red, green, and yellow paint.*

Pallet is a flat platform on which goods are loaded.
*Several **pallets** at the warehouse contain new DVD players.*

Palm off, Pawn off

Palm off, meaning to deceive or defraud someone with something inferior, is the correct expression. The phrase probably originated with magicians, who typically use their palms to hide items during tricks.
*They had no right to **palm off** those damaged school buses on the other school districts.*

Paltry, Petty

Paltry means meager, trivial, or measly.
*The company made a **paltry** contribution to the fund this year.*

Petty means minor, trifling, or of little importance.
*The rules apply in **petty** offenses and other misdemeanor cases.*

Pamphlet, Brochure, Leaflet

*See entry for **Brochure, Leaflet, Pamphlet**.*

Parameter, Perimeter

Parameter is a quantity or mathematical variable that stays constant.
*The applet is modified by using the **parameters** in the file.*

Perimeter is the outer boundary of an area.
*The dog never leaves the **perimeter** of the yard.*

Paramount, Tantamount

Paramount means primary or top.
*Customer satisfaction is the **paramount** concern of our staff.*

Tantamount means equivalent to or the same as.
*The general's action is **tantamount** to a declaration of peace.*

Paraplegic, Hemiplegic, Quadriplegic

*See entry for **Hemiplegic, Paraplegic, Quadriplegic**.*

Parlay, Parley

Parlay means to bet one's winnings over again. It can also mean to exploit something into something more valuable.
*He **parlayed** his blackjack winnings into enough money to pay for all his expenses.*
*Using an infomercial, he **parlayed** a simple invention into a national bestseller.*

Parley, as a verb, means to confer with an enemy, to negotiate, or to discuss.
*The leaders plan to **parley** their differences in a neutral location.*

Parley, as a noun, refers to a conference to resolve disagreements or disputes.
*The two leaders agreed to meet for a **parley**.*

Partake, Participate

You **partake** of something and you **participate** in something.
*After **participating** in the tournament, we wanted to **partake** of some refreshments.*

Partially, Partly

Partially means to a certain degree or extent.
*The company **partially** shut down for two weeks to save energy.*

Partly means not completely.
*Doctors feel genetics can be **partly** to blame for mental illness.*

Passable, Passible

Passable means barely satisfactory or able to be passed.
We sat through a passable performance of "Hamlet" last night.
Whether the roads are passable depends on the weather.

Passible, a theological term, means capable of feeling or suffering.
Some believe that God does suffer and is therefore passible.

Passed, Past

Passed is the past tense of *pass*.
The House and Senate passed electronic signature bills.
We passed that town on the way to St. Louis.

Past refers to time or distance (and can never be a verb).
The film covers computer history, from the past to the present.
We drove past that store yesterday.

Passport, Visa

A **passport** is an official government document that certifies a person's identity and citizenship and permits travel to another country. A **visa** is an official authorization stamped on a passport that permits a person's entry into and travel within a country.

Pastoral, Pastorial

Pastoral is the correct word.

Pathos, Bathos

See entry for Bathos, Pathos.

Patience, Patients

Patience refers to the ability to wait.
Patience is a virtue we should all practice.

Patients are people under medical treatment.
Most patients can expect some relief within two to four days.

Peaceable, Peaceful

Peaceable means inclined to peace.
*The men met in a **peaceable** spirit to resolve their differences.*

Peaceful means tranquil.
*We are committed to making a safe and **peaceful** environment.*

Peak, Peek, Pique

Peak, as a noun, means summit; as a verb, it means maximize.
*Those records show Gracie is at the **peak** of her running career.*
*At what age did you **peak** in your running career?*

Peek means to peep or snoop.
***Peek** into the window to see if Karol and Jo have left the house.*

Pique means to excite or irritate.
*Did you **pique** his interest with your sales pitch?*
*After hearing those comments, Ed is definitely **piqued**.*

*The climber **piqued** his interest by **peeking** at the mountain **peak** through his telescope.*

Peccable, Peccant

Peccable means capable of sinning.
*"A frail and **peccable** mortal."*—Sir Walter Scott

Peccant means guilty of sinning.
*Opening the skull to relieve **peccant** humors was once common.*

Penultimate, Ultimate

Penultimate means next to last.
*Next week is the **penultimate** week of the fall semester.*

Ultimate means last or superlative.
*The **ultimate** fate of Atlantis is unknown.*
*Mary prepared the **ultimate** apple pie for my birthday.*

People, Persons

People and **persons** are generally interchangeable, but **people** is the preferred word. **Persons** may be considered overly formal or haughty.

Per say, Per se

Per se, meaning as such or intrinsically, is the correct phrase.
*Partisanship **per se** does not preclude political action.*

Percent, Percentage, Percentage point

Percent is specific and is usually used with a number.
*They expect to reduce their workforce by 15 **percent**.*

Percentage is not specific and is never used with a number.
*The reduction affects a small **percentage** of engineers.*

Note: **Percent** should be spelled as one word (not **per cent**).
Also, **percent** is becoming accepted without a number by it.
*What **percent** of your workday is spent in meetings?*

Percentage point is the correct phrase when referring to a change in a figure that is already a percentage. One percentage point is always 1/100th of the total.
*The President's approval rating fell from 43 percent to 40 percent, a drop of three **percentage points** (not 3 percent).*

Perenial, Annals, Annual

A **perennial** is a plant that grows for many years. **Annals** is a compiled record of events. An **annual** is a plant that grows for just one year (or season).

Perfume, Cologne

Perfume is a strong, relatively expensive fragrance. **Cologne** is a weak, relatively inexpensive fragrance.

Periodic, Sporadic

Periodic means occurring at regular or predictable intervals.
*Lisa told us she would be having **periodic** performance reviews.*

Sporadic means occurring at irregular or unpredictable times.
*Some western states are experiencing **sporadic** power outages.*

Perpetrate, Perpetuate

Perpetrate means being responsible for something.
*Bill likes to **perpetrate** practical jokes on his teammates.*

Perpetuate means cause to be remembered or last indefinitely.
*The Vietnam Memorial **perpetuates** the memory of those killed in that war.*

Perquisite, Prerequisite

Perquisite refers to a special benefit or privilege (a **perq**).
*A new company car is a **perquisite** for all their executives.*

Prerequisite refers to something required in advance.
*What **prerequisite** course does the college require for admission to this program?*

Persecute, Prosecute

Persecute means to harass or treat unjustly.
*The committee may **persecute** them for their political dissent.*

Prosecute means to bring legal action against or to pursue something until the end.
*Some states **prosecute** juveniles as adults in criminal court.*
*Their patent **prosecution** on DNA techniques helped the industry.*

Person that, Person who

Person who is the preferred phrase in formal writing. Some purists reserve **who** for people and **that** for animals or things.
*Jeff is the **person who** chose engineering as a career.*
*That's the elephant **that** almost lost its memory.*

Personal, Personnel

Personal means private.
*My date did not want to discuss **personal** matters.*

Personnel means a group of people, usually all of whom are part of the same organization.
*We have the qualified **personnel** to get the job done.*
*The **Personnel** Department handles the employee's exit interview.*

Perspective, Prospective

Perspective is a point of view or a way to create the illusion of depth in a drawing or painting.
*From the teacher's **perspective**, it is another way of learning.*
*The painting shows a three-dimensional **perspective** of Toronto.*

Prospective means probable.
*The **prospective** buyer went to the website to learn more.*

Perspicacious, Perspicuous

Perspicacious means having a quick understanding of things.
*Anand is a **perspicacious** student of law.*

Perspicuous means presenting things clearly and precisely.
*Their account of the events is quite **perspicuous** to everyone.*

Persuade, Convince

See entry for **Convince, Persuade**.

Pertinence, Impertinence

See entry for **Impertinence, Pertinence**.

Peruse, Skim

Peruse means to examine or read carefully.

*They want to **peruse** the contract thoroughly before signing it.*

*From the **prospective** student's **perspective**, the rowdy campus looked great.*

Skim means glance over or read quickly.
*He intended to **skim** the material right before the meeting.*

Perverbial, Proverbial
Proverbial is the correct word.

Phase, Faze
*See entry for **Faze, Phase**.*

Phenomena, Phenomenon
Phenomena is the plural form of the noun **phenomenon**.
*Such **phenomena** are difficult to comprehend and explain.*
*Many sightings continue to fuel the UFO **phenomenon**.*

Philippinos, Filipinos
People of the Philippines are referred to as **Filipinos**.

Physician, Doctor
Physician is a general term for a doctor of medicine, someone legally qualified to practice medicine. **Doctor** refers to anyone who has been granted a doctor's degree. All physicians are doctors of medicine, but not all doctors practice medicine.

Picaresque, Picturesque
Picaresque refers to adventurers or clever rogues.
*Twain's "Tom Sawyer" contains many **picaresque** characters.*

Picturesque refers to being attractive or pretty.
*Lake Placid contains some wonderful **picturesque** views.*

Pitfall, Pratfall
A **pitfall** is an unexpected danger.
*The mercenary encountered many **pitfalls** while fighting rebels.*

A **pratfall** is a comical or humiliating fall, often used in physical humor.
*The kindergartners laughed uproariously at the clown's **pratfalls**.*

Plaintiff, Plaintive

Plaintiff refers to one who brings a suit into a court of law.
*The **plaintiff** claimed the defendant scratched his new Mercedes.*

Plaintive refers to being mournful or melancholy.
*A **plaintive** cry for help could be heard in the distance.*

Plan for, Plan it, Plan on, Plan to

Plan on is incorrect grammar. Use *plan for*, *plan it*, or *plan to*.
*Please **plan to** attend our next chapter meeting.*

Plaque, Tartar

Plaque is a thin film of mucus and bacteria on a tooth's surface.
Tartar (also called dental calculus) is a hard, yellowish plaque that collects food particles and salt deposits.

Playwright, Playwrite

Someone who writes plays is called a **playwright**, not a **playwrite**.

Plenitude, Plentitude

Plenitude is preferred in American usage.

Plethora, Dearth

*See entry for **Dearth, Plethora**.*

Plum, Plumb

Plum is the juicy fruit.
*In the summer, I could eat **plums** all day.*

Plumb means to explore something fully.
*He **plumbed** the depths of inner-city life for his new novel.*

Plurality, Majority

*See entry for **Majority, Plurality**.*

Podium, Lectern, Pulpit, Rostrum

*See entry for **Lectern, Podium, Pulpit, Rostrum**.*

Pole, Poll

Pole refers to a long staff (***totem pole***) or to either extremity of a sphere's axis (*South Pole*).
*Four **poles** supported the large banquet tent.*
*On January 18, 1912, Captain Robert Scott, an English explorer, reached the **South Pole**.*

Poll refers to the casting of votes in an election or a survey of public opinion.
*Few run for public office today without relying on opinion **polls**.*

Polygamy, Monogamy, Bigamy

Bigamy means being married to just two spouses at the same time; **monogamy** means being married to only one person; **polygamy** means having multiple spouses at the same time.

Pomace, Pumice

Pomace refers to the solid remains of fruit or vegetables after a pressing.
*The tomato **pomace** that was prepared is great in tomato sauce.*

Pumice refers to a light, volcanic stone often ground for use as a polishing agent.
*The stone finishers used a fine **pumice** to polish the stone.*

Pom-pom, Pompon

Pom-pom is a lightweight, automatic weapon. **Pompon** is what a cheerleader waves.

Pool table, Billiards table

Unlike a **pool** table, a **billiards** table has no pockets.

Populace, Populous

Populace, a noun, refers to the common people or population.
*The city of Los Angeles has a huge and still growing **populace**.*

Populous, an adjective, means densely populated.
*San Diego is a **populous** and growing southern California city.*

Popular, Common, Mutual, Ordinary
*See entry for **Common, Mutual, Ordinary, Popular**.*

Pore, Pour
Pore as a verb means to study or examine something. As a noun, it means a tiny opening in the skin or the leaves of a plant.
*The HR department **pored** over the many job applications.*
*The **pores** of his skin tend to clog easily.*

Pour as a verb means to flow freely or to empty a fluid from one source to another.
*Please **pour** water into all the glasses.*

Port, Harbor
A **port** is a place where ships load and unload their cargo. A **harbor** is a body of water that protects ships.

Port, Bow, Starboard, Stern
*See entry for **Bow, Port, Starboard, Stern**.*

Portend, Pretend
Portend means to indicate beforehand.
*An increase in downsizing could **portend** a tough job market.*

Pretend means to make believe, profess, or disguise.
*Children like to **pretend** sometimes that they are adults.*

Portion, Apportion, Proportion
*See entry for **Apportion, Portion, Proportion**.*

Possible, Probable
Possible means it could happen or be done.
*It's **possible** the hurricane could hit New York by next week.*

Probable means it is likely to happen.
*It's **probable** the hurricane will hit the Carolina coast today.*

Posterity, Prosperity

Posterity refers to all of a person's descendants.
*He lived meagerly so his **posterity** could enjoy a better life.*

Prosperity refers to wealth or success.
*After the factory was built, the city enjoyed a new **prosperity**.*

Postpone, Cancel, Delay

*See entry for **Cancel, Delay, Postpone**.*

Practicable, Practical

Practicable means capable of being put into practice.
*Considering the budget, is it **practicable** to build a new arena?*

Practical means useful, sensible, or worth being put into practice.
*The plan contains **practical** measures for improving traffic flow.*

Pragmatic, Dogmatic

*See entry for **Dogmatic, Pragmatic**.*

Precede, Proceed

Precede means to go before something.
*The national anthem **precedes** all of our baseball games.*

Proceed means to go ahead with an action.
*Click here if you wish to **proceed** to the next step.*

Precedence, Precedents

Precedence refers to priority, rank, or an act of coming before.
*The need for safety took **precedence** over all other matters.*

Precedents refers to previous actions that serve as examples.
*A few decisions established **precedents** for the pursuit of justice.*

Precipitate, Precipitous

Precipitate, as an adjective, means rash or sudden.
*Their **precipitate** entry into the dot com market led to a disaster.*

Precipitous means very steep.
*Video conferencing is leading to a **precipitous** decline in travel.*

Preclude, Prelude

Preclude means to make impossible or to rule out.
*Her sore throat will **preclude** her from singing tonight.*

Prelude is an action that acts as an introduction to an event.
*Their actions seemed to be an ironic **prelude** to disaster.*

Prelude is also a short musical selection that serves to introduce a larger musical selection.
*The orchestra played the **prelude** promptly at 8 p.m.*

Predominant, Predominate

Predominant, an adjective, means the most common or conspicuous.
*The **predominant** view is that he is the best athlete ever.*

Predominate, a verb, means to prevail or wield greater power or quantity.
*The good will of the people definitely **predominates** in this town.*

Note: Older dictionaries list the words as synonyms if used as adjectives.

Preface, Foreword, Introduction

*See entry for **Foreword, Introduction, Preface**.*

Premature, Immature

*See entry for **Immature, Premature**.*

Premier, Premiere

Premier, as an adjective, means first in importance. As a noun, it means a chief government executive.
*That is one of the **premier** magazines on the newsstands today.*
*The **premier** of that country invited us to his palace for dinner.*

Premiere means opening night or first public showing.
*We attended the **premiere** of "The Phantom of the Opera".*

Premise, Premises

Premise refers to an assumption or a supposition.
*He understands the basic **premise** of public relations.*

Premises refers to a house, building, grounds, or other property.
*Finding the right office **premises** may improve productivity.*

Prescribe, Proscribe

Prescribe means to set down a rule or to order something.
*The labor law **prescribes** a standard 40-hour workweek.*
*Perhaps the doctor can **prescribe** a more effective drug.*

Proscribe means to condemn, forbid, or prohibit something.
*The Food and Drug Administration **proscribed** Laetrile years ago.*

Presentiment, Presentment

Presentiment means premonition.
*The studio has a **presentiment** that the film will be a success.*

A **presentment** is something exhibited or presented.
*She reimburses you upon **presentment** of a signed receipt.*

Press, Click, Type

*See entry for **Click, Press, Type**.*

Presume, Assume

*See entry for **Assume, Presume**.*

Presumptive, Presumptuous

Presumptive means presumed.
*Smith is the **presumptive** new CEO, though he hasn't been promoted yet.*

Presumptuous means arrogant, bold, or forward.
*It is **presumptuous** of them to invite themselves to our party.*

Pretense, Pretext

Pretense is a false claim or a show of insincere behavior.
*The drug should not be legalized under any **pretense**.*
*The compliments we received were all **pretense**.*

Pretext is the professed purpose for something, usually false.
*Mark lost his job under the **pretext** of being overqualified.*

Prevaricate, Procrastinate, Equivocate

*See entry for **Equivocate, Prevaricate, Procrastinate**.*

Prevent, Hinder

*See entry for **Hinder, Prevent**.*

Preventative, Preventive

Preventive is the preferred spelling, but either is acceptable.
__Preventive__ dentistry measures can lead to healthier smiles.

Principal, Principle

Principal, as an adjective, means foremost. As a noun, it is the head of a school or the amount of money borrowed.
Who are the __principal__ developers of the new hardware product?
The middle school is getting a new __principal__ for the fall.
The mortgage payment includes both __principal__ and interest.

Principle is a noun that refers to law or personal conviction.
It works on the __principle__ that warm air rises.
It is against our basic __principles__ to make such a statement.

Prison, Jail

A **prison**, sometimes referred to as a *penitentiary*, is a long-term detaining facility for those convicted of major offenses. A **jail** is a short-term detaining facility for those awaiting trial or for those convicted of minor offenses.

Problem, Dilemma, Quandary

*See entry for **Dilemma, Problem, Quandary**.*

Problematic, Problemsome

Problematic is the correct word despite the existence of words such as *fearsome, troublesome,* and *worrisome*.

Procrastinate, Equivocate, Prevaricate

*See entry for **Equivocate, Prevaricate, Procrastinate**.*

Prodigy, Progeny, Protégé, Protégée

Prodigy refers to a person with exceptional talents.
*Many musicians consider Mozart a child **prodigy**.*

Progeny refers to offspring, children, descendant, or followers.
*After her brother's death, she is the last **progeny** of her parents.*

Protégé is a male who is guided or helped by someone.
*As a youth, Justin considered himself a **protégé** of Buddy Holly.*

Protégée is a female who is guided or helped by someone.
*Loretta was a **protégée** of Jane, the head accountant.*

Prognosis, Diagnosis

*See entry for **Diagnosis, Prognosis**.*

Prohibit, Forbid

*See entry for **Forbid, Prohibit**.*

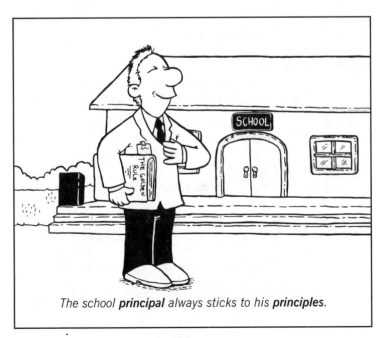

*The school **principal** always sticks to his **principles**.*

Proletariat, Bourgeois

Proletariat refers to the lower class. **Bourgeois** refers to the middle class.

Prone, Prostate, Prostrate, Supine

Prone means lying face down.
*The old man enjoys sleeping in the **prone** position.*

Prostate refers to the male gland.
*The doctor recommends having a yearly **prostate** exam.*

Prostrate also means lying face down (often after an accident) or overcome with grief.
*The football player lies **prostrate** after the tackle.*
*Understandably, she was **prostrate** with much grief.*

Supine means lying face up.
*The beach is full of sun worshippers, **supine** on the sand.*

Proof, Evidence

*See entry for **Evidence, Proof**.*

Prophecy, Prophesy

Prophecy, a noun, means a prediction.
*Is there a **prophecy** in that book that could be fulfilled this year?*

Prophesy, a verb, means to predict by divine inspiration.
*What did they **prophesy** about our future on earth?*

Protagonist, Antagonist

*See entry for **Antagonist, Protagonist**.*

Protean, Protein

Protean means versatile or capable of taking on varied shapes or meanings.
*Robert De Niro has shown his **protean** talent in many films.*

Protein is an organic compound essential for living cells.
*Nutritionists say high-**protein** diets may pose a risk to health.*

Proved, Proven

Proved, a verb, means to establish the truth of something.
*Inconsistencies in the man's testimony **proved** he was lying.*

Proven, a past participle of *prove*, is used only as an adjective.
*Hypnosis is a **proven** and popular method for quitting smoking.*

Prudent, Prudish

Prudent means exercising good common sense or judgment.
*It was **prudent** of them to invest with the company when they did.*

Prudish means very formal, precise, or reserved.
*Our company is too **prudish** to introduce a relaxed dress code.*

Pseudo, Quasi

Pseudo is a prefix meaning false, counterfeit, or deceptive. It requires a hyphen when joined to a proper noun.
*The **pseudo**science didn't impress the potential investors.*
*The **pseudo**-European furniture, made in China, sold well.*

Quasi is a prefix meaning resembling or in some manner. It is usually hyphenated.
*The **quasi**-scientific literature presented little bona fide research.*

Purposefully, Purposely

Purposefully means to act with determination or purpose.
*The coach strode **purposefully** to the TV booth for an interview.*

Purposely means to do something deliberately or intentionally.
*Please do not remove those books—I put them there **purposely**.*

Q

"One should not aim at being possible to understand, but at being impossible to misunderstand."—Quintillian

Quadriplegic, Hemiplegic, Paraplegic

See entry for **Hemiplegic, Paraplegic, Quadriplegic.**

Qualitative, Quantitative

Qualitative refers to the characteristics or properties of quality, and **quantitative** refers to the measure of something. **Qualitative** data is information that is not clearly quantifiable, such as a scientist's observations, the taste of something, or a videotape of an interview. **Quantitative** data can be counted, such as the temperature of a liquid, the number of petals on a flower, or the amount of salt in a gallon of seawater.

Quarrel, Argument

See entry for **Argument, Quarrel.**

Quash, Squash

Quash, which typically refers to legal action, means to annul or invalidate.
*Censorship rules permit the authorities to **quash** almost anything.*

Squash means to crush, squeeze, or suppress.
*If they had aspirations of winning, their efforts were **squashed**.*

Quasi, Pseudo

See entry for **Pseudo, Quasi.**

Quell, Quench

Quell means to pacify, suppress, or put down with force.
*The new fiscal policies failed to **quell** the economic fears.*

Quench means to cool, extinguish, or satisfy.
*Some people use tea rather than water to **quench** their thirst.*

Queue, Cue

*See entry for **Cue, Queue**.*

Quiet, Quite

Quiet means silence.
*"All **Quiet** on the Western Front" is the first antiwar film with sound.*

Quite means really or close.
*The banana could **quite** possibly be the world's perfect food.*
*Jeb wasn't **quite** the right person for this assignment.*

Quotation, Quote

Quotation, a noun, refers to words someone said.
*The **quotations** of JFK and Churchill continue to be popular.*

Quote, a verb, means to repeat the words of someone.
*Do you mind if the press **quotes** you on that statement?*

Note: Used informally, **quote** is the shortened word for **quotation**.
*The online service offers a daily **quote** on all stock prices.*
*That movie has many memorable **quotes**.*

R

"Scarcely any of our intellectual operations could be carried on to any considerable extent without the agency of words."—Peter Roget

Rabble rouser, Rebel rouser

Rabble rouser, an agitator, is the correct expression. The phrase first appeared in England in the mid-19th century as a combination of *rabble* and *rouse*.
*A group of **rabble rousers** disrupted the football game.*

Rack, Wrack

Rack and **wrack** both mean to strain or torment. Prefer **rack**.
*We are **racking** our brains to remember the name of that song.*

Rancor, Ranker

Rancor refers to long-lasting bitterness or hatred.
*The explosive testimony brought even more courtroom **rancor**.*

Ranker refers to a person with an official position or grade.
*The paper says he was only a middle **ranker** and not a senior military leader.*

Rapport, Rapore

Rapport, meaning to have a positive relationship with someone, is the correct word.

Rapt, Wrapped

Rapt means carried away or wholly absorbed.
*They watched the mine rescue with **rapt** attention.*

Wrapped means to bundle, cover, or enclose.
*"A man **wrapped** up in himself makes a very small bundle."*
—Benjamin Franklin

Rare, Unprecedented

Rare means uncommon or unusual.
*Exposure to uranium is a **rare** cause of lung cancer.*

Unprecedented means without previous example.
*They faced a refugee crisis on an **unprecedented** scale.*

Rarely ever

Avoid this phrase. Just use **rarely** by itself.
***Rarely** (not **rarely ever**) do we hire someone without a degree.*

Rational, Rationale

Rational, an adjective, means having or exercising the ability to reason.
*Is it **rational** to believe that life exists on other planets?*

Rationale, a noun, refers to an explanation or basic reason.
*We do not understand the **rationale** for selling the business.*

Raucous, Ruckus

Raucous, an adjective, means loud or rambunctious.
*It's not unusual for them to throw a **raucous** party once a month.*

Ruckus, a noun, means a fight, disturbance, or commotion.
*Authorities are more interested in stopping the **ruckus** than in finding the culprit.*

Ravage, Ravish

Ravage means to destroy or devastate something.
*Fires continued to **ravage** the western states for many weeks.*

Ravish means to carry off by force or overwhelm with emotion.
*In the novel, the king's daughter was **ravished** by her captors.*
*The beauty of the Canadian sunset **ravished** the travelers.*

Rebound, Redound

Rebound means to bounce or spring back.
*The company's stock price **rebounded** after the news hit.*

Redound means to contribute or lead to something.
*Her exceptional performance **redounds** to the company's benefit.*

Rebuff, Rebut, Refute, Repudiate

Rebuff means to snub or reject someone.
*We offered to help with the cleanup, but he **rebuffed** us.*

Rebut means to argue against something.
*Unless the board **rebuts** the proposal, the idea is accepted.*

Refute means to prove something is false.
*The defense team **refuted** much of the earlier testimony.*

Repudiate means to reject or refuse something.
*We were always taught to **repudiate** discrimination and violence.*

Recapitulate, Capitulate

*See entry for **Capitulate, Recapitulate**.*

Recital, Concert

*See entry for **Concert, Recital**.*

Recourse, Resort

Recourse refers to turning to someone or something for help.
*What **recourse** do online shoppers have today?*

Resort, as a noun, is something you turn to after all other options have failed. **Resort**, as a verb, means to have recourse.
*As a last **resort**, I contacted the police.*
*Because of the accident, he had to **resort** to riding his bike.*

Recur, Reoccur

Recur is the preferred word.

Redoubtable, Indubitable, Undoubted

*See entry for **Indubitable, Redoubtable, Undoubted**.*

Reeking havoc, Wreaking havoc

Wreaking havoc is the correct phrase.
*The power surges are **wreaking havoc** with our new computer.*

Refer, Allude, Elude

See entry for **Allude, Elude, Refer**.

Refrain, Restrain

Refrain means to choose not to do something or partake of something.
*The students were asked to **refrain** from leaving class early.*

Restrain means to immobilize by force or forbid an action.
*The nurses had to **restrain** the patient in order to avoid injury.*

Refugee, Evacuee

See entry for **Evacuee, Refugee**.

Regardless, Irregardless

See entry for **Irregardless, Regardless**.

Regime, Regimen, Regiment

Regime, a noun, refers to a government, usually an authoritarian one.
*The country underwent **regime** change on its own terms.*

Regimen, a noun, refers to a therapeutic treatment, usually including diet and exercise.
*The benefits of a daily fitness **regimen** are endless.*

Regiment, as a noun, refers to a military unit or large group of people; as a verb, it means to direct or command.
*The people's good wishes went to the soldiers of our **regiment**.*
*They sought to **regiment** the people and their property.*

Regretfully, Regrettably

Regretfully means with feelings of regret.
*Prior commitments made him **regretfully** decline the invitation.*

Regrettably means unfortunately.
*It looked like the rain would stop, but **regrettably** it did not.*

Reign, Rein

Royalty can **reign** (rule), and a horse has **reins** to pull to stop it.

Reiterate, Iterate

These synonyms mean *to repeat*.

Reknown, Renown

Renown, meaning fame, is the correct word. **Reknown** is not a word.

Relegate, Delegate

*See entry for **Delegate, Relegate**.*

Reluctant, Reticent

Reluctant means opposing or unwilling to act.
*Few golfers are **reluctant** to wear soft spikes on the course.*

Reticent means keeping silent or unwilling to speak freely.
*Her **reticent** nature conceals many of her talents.*

Remarkable, Marked

*See entry for **Marked, Remarkable**.*

Remediable, Remedial

Remediable means capable of being corrected or remedied.
*Dr. Watson assures us your teeth problems are **remediable**.*

Remedial means supplying a remedy.
*A research brief on **remedial** education is available at the office.*

Remiss, Amiss

*See entry for **Amiss, Remiss**.*

Remuneration, Renumeration

The correct word is **remuneration** meaning compensation (money).
*Executive **remuneration** is the focus of considerable attention.*

Renounce, Denounce

*See entry for **Denounce, Renounce**.*

Repertoire, Repertory

Repertoire is the range of entertainment a person or group performs.
*Larry has a good **repertoire** of corny jokes that we enjoy.*

Repertory is the place where a person or group performs.
*The Owego Drama Players have their own **repertory** theatre.*

Represented, Representated

Representated is not a word.

Repress, Oppress

*See entry for **Repress, Oppress**.*

Reputation, Character

*See entry for **Character, Reputation**.*

Request, Behest

*See entry for **Behest, Request**.*

Resident, Citizen

A **resident** lives in a community but doesn't necessarily have the rights of a citizen. A **citizen** is someone who has the full rights of a nation, either by birth or naturalization.

Resister, Resistor

Resister is anyone who offers resistance. **Resistor** is a device that controls current in an electrical circuit.

Respectably, Respectfully, Respectively

Respectably means in a decent way.
*All of the invitees are dressed **respectably** for the occasion.*

Respectfully means in a courteous way.
*Tom **respectfully** submitted his opinion to the city council.*

Respectively means in the order given or indicated.
*Harold and Ted are an engineer and lawyer, **respectively**.*

Restive, Restless

Restive means impatient or fidgety under pressure or restraint.
*The guards are worried about the **restive** prisoners.*

Restless means uneasy, unquiet, or unable to rest or relax.
*The doctor felt her **restless** nights were due to sleep apnea.*

Retch, Wretch

Retch refers to vomiting or gagging; **wretch** refers to a pitiable or groveling person.

Retroactive from, Retroactive to

Retroactive to is the preferred phrase.
*The salary increases are **retroactive to** January 1.*

Revenge, Avenge

*See entry for **Avenge, Revenge.***

Review, Revue

Review refers to critically evaluating.
*Her new movie has received mixed **reviews** from the critics.*

Revue refers to a musical or theatrical production.
*Igor Stravinsky once composed a ballet score for a Broadway **revue**.*

Revolve, Rotate

These words are synonyms in everyday writing but not in scientific or technical writing.
*The earth **revolves** around the sun and **rotates** upon its axis.*

Reward, Award

*See entry for **Award, Reward.***

Riffle, Rifle

Riffle means to browse or thumb through something.
*She **riffled** the class material just before the test.*

Rifle means to ransack or steal something.
*Someone **rifled** through their house while they were out of town.*

Right, Wright

Right means morally, legally, or properly.
*The umpire did the **right** thing when he admitted his mistake.*

Wright is a maker such as a playwright.
*Many people consider Neil Simon a famous American **wright**.*

Rightfully, Rightly

Rightfully means having a claim or right to something.
*Marty is **rightfully** the owner of the rare painting.*

Rightly means correctly or properly.
*Joe **rightly** refuses to sign a contract until an accord is reached.*

Rigorous, Vigorous

Rigorous means harsh, precise, severe, or strict.
*The senior class underwent a **rigorous** training course.*

Vigorous means energetic, robust, or strong.
*Some dentists say teeth do not need **vigorous** brushing.*

Robbery, Burglary, Theft

*See entry for **Burglary, Robbery, Theft**.*

Rostrum, Podium, Pulpit, Lectern

*See entry for **Lectern, Podium, Pulpit, Rostrum**.*

S

"My words fly up, my thoughts remain below: Words without thoughts never to heaven go."—William Shakespeare

Sachet, Sashay

Sachet is a small packet of perfumed powder.
*While drying clothes, Jo dropped a small **sachet** in the dryer.*

Sashay means to strut or flounce.
*After their victory, the girls proudly **sashayed** around the field.*

Safe-deposit box, Safety deposit box

Safe-deposit box is the correct phrase.

Salacious, Salubrious

Salacious means lecherous, lustful, or obscene.
*We all receive **salacious**, virus-bearing e-mail.*

Salubrious means conducive or favorable to health and well-being.
*Every winter they enjoy the **salubrious** weather in Florida.*

Salon, Saloon

A **salon** is a large room usually used for entertaining people, cutting hair, or exhibiting artwork. A **saloon** is a place where alcoholic beverages are sold.

Sanguinary, Sanguine

Sanguinary means bloody or murderous.
*The Battle of Gettysburg was the most **sanguinary** battle ever fought on this continent.*

Sanguine means cheerful, optimistic, or confident.
*She is **sanguine** about the future and happy to have a new job.*

Sarcastic, Skeptical, Cynical
*See entry for **Cynical, Sarcastic, Skeptical**.*

Saving, Savings
Saving refers to something preserved.
*With the new process, we realized a **saving** of two hours.*

Use **savings** when referring to banks, bank accounts, and bonds.
*We opened a **savings** account that yields a high interest rate.*
*John won a $100 **savings** bond in the speech contest.*

Note: One would never write, "*a losses of $20*", so one should not write, "*a savings of $20*".
*The girl invested her **saving** of $500 in a **savings** bond.*

Scale, Octave
A **scale** is a series of eight notes played in alphabetical order.
Octave is the distance covered by any eight notes of a scale.

Scapegoat, Escape goat
Scapegoat, which is one who is blamed for another's misdeeds, is the correct word, though **escape goat** is actually closer to the original meaning of the phrase. It has roots in an ancient Jewish custom that allows one of two sacrificial goats to go free, taking the sins of the people with it. This goat was the *escaped goat*, which was later shortened to **scapegoat**.
*Making Jim the **scapegoat** for the team's loss is absurd.*

Scarcely than, Scarcely when
Scarcely when is the correct expression.
*We **scarcely** moved our car **when** we were stopped by the police.*

Schilling, Shilling
Schilling is Austrian currency and **shilling** is British currency.

Scrupulous, Meticulous
*See entry for **Meticulous, Scrupulous**.*

Scull, Skull

Scull is an oar used by a rower.
*Dan and Ben are propelling their new canoe with heavy **sculls**.*

Skull is the bone that protects the brain and face.
*You can get a slight **skull** fracture and sometimes not realize it.*

Seasonable, Seasonal

Seasonable means appropriate for the season or occasion.
*The sleet is unexpected but **seasonable** for this time of year.*

Seasonal refers to a particular season.
*Her **seasonal** work includes giving golf lessons in Miami.*

*Fred knew they were in trouble when his **scull** hit a **skull**.*

Sectarian, Secular

Sectarian refers to sects or to religious groups.
*His message was a **sectarian** appeal to help others get funding.*

Secular means not connected to a religion.
*Although identified as a **secular** charity, it will get some donations from the church.*

Seeing as, Seeing that

Avoid these phrases in writing. Use *because* instead.
***Because** (not **seeing as** or **seeing that**) our car broke down, we missed our starting time.*

Seize the day, Cease the day

Seize the day is the correct phrase.

Semiannual

Synonym for *biannual* (twice a year). *See entry for **Biannual, Biennial**.*

Semimonthly, Bimonthly

*See entry for **Bimonthly, Semimonthly**.*

Sensor, Censer, Censor, Censure

*See entry for **Censer, Censor, Censure, Sensor**.*

Sensual, Sensuous

Sensual means physically gratifying to the body or its senses.
*She delighted in the **sensual** warmth of the Hawaiian Islands.*

Sensuous means appealing to the senses.
*Her music is not only warm and **sensuous**, but relaxing as well.*

Serve, Service

Generally, people are **served** and things are **serviced**.
*She was elected to congress to **serve** the people's interest.*
*He gained car owner confidence by delivering quality **service**.*

Session, Cession

See entry for Cession, Session.

Sewage, Sewerage

Sewage is the waste that goes through the **sewerage**. Although **sewage** lines is okay, **sewerage** lines is considered redundant.

Sex, Gender

Sex refers to biological differences: chromosomes, hormonal profiles, and internal and external sex organs. **Gender** describes the characteristics that a society or culture delineates as masculine or feminine.

Shade, Hue, Tint

See entry for Hue, Shade, Tint.

Shall, Will

Today in everyday American business writing and speaking, the *wills* out number the *shalls*. Few people distinguish between them anymore. But if you are a traditionalist, here are the rules for handling **shall** and **will**:

Shall is used for the first-person future tense.
*We **shall** enjoy working for the new town supervisor.*

Will is used for the second and third-person future tense.
*You (They) **will** enjoy working for the new town supervisor.*

For legal documents and some government contracts, **shall** expresses determination or a guarantee, and **will** expresses a plan to do something. Either word can be used for first-, second-, or third-person pronouns in the future tense.
*We (You, They) **shall** supply the required documentation when requested by the customer.*
*Before the end of the month, the supervisor **will** appraise all of her employees.*

Shanty, Chantey

See entry for Chantey, Shanty.

Shear, Sheer

Shear means to cut or clip.
*He knows how to **shear** a sheep correctly.*

Sheer means fine, transparent, or complete.
*The **sheer** drapes failed to block any of the light.*
*It was just **sheer** luck they won the game.*

Sherbet, Sherbert, Sorbet

Use **sherbet** (with one *r*) not **sherbert** when referring to the milk-based confection. **Sorbet** is a fancy fruit-based iced dessert.

Should have, Should of

Should have is the correct phrase.
*They **should have** come downstairs earlier.*

Shudder, Shutter

Shudder means to vibrate, shake, or shiver from fear, revulsion, or cold.
*The severe air turbulence caused the airplane to **shudder**.*
*I **shudder** to imagine where we will be if the measure fails.*

Shutter is a screen or cover, or a movable cover for a window.
*A camera's **shutter** is similar to a person's eyelid.*
*Jill closed the window **shutters** during the storm.*

Shudder to think, Shutter to think

Shudder to think is the correct expression.

Sight, Site, Cite

*See entry for **Cite, Sight, Site**.*

Silicon, Silicone

Silicon is the nonmetallic chemical element used in microchips.
*The technician put the **silicon** wafer into the slot.*

Silicone is plastic and other materials that contain silicon.
***Silicone** is widely used as a protective coating for shoes.*

Simile, Metaphor

Simile and **metaphor** are comparisons that are quite different, but are commonly confused simply because they are so similar. A **simile** is an approximation that uses the words *like* or *as*. (*A good book is like a good meal.*) A **metaphor** is a definitive comparison that does not use the words *like* or *as*. (*A wire is a road for electrons.*)

*Jessica **shuddered** by the open **shutters**.*

Simple, Simplistic

Simple means plain, not complex, or uncomplicated.
*Joe's explanation is quite **simple** and easy to comprehend.*

Simplistic means unrealistically simple and usually used in a derogatory sense.
*Bob's explanation is quite **simplistic** and omits many key points.*

Simulate, Emulate

*See entry for **Emulate, Simulate**.*

Sinecure, Cynosure

*See entry for **Cynosure, Sinecure**.*

Sister-in-laws, Sisters-in-law

Sisters-in-law is the correct phrase.

Site, Cite, Sight

*See entry for **Cite, Sight, Site**.*

Skeptical, Cynical, Sarcastic

*See entry for **Cynical, Sarcastic, Skeptical**.*

Sketch, Skit

Though both are short, entertaining presentations, a **sketch** is usually serious and unrehearsed while a **skit** is typically rehearsed and comical.

Skiddish, Skittish

Skittish is the correct word.

Skim, Peruse

*See entry for **Peruse, Skim**.*

Slander, Liable, Libel, Lible

*See entry for **Liable, Libel, Lible, Slander**.*

Sleight of hand, Slight of hand
Sleight of hand is the correct expression.

Slither of cake, Sliver of cake
Sliver of cake is the correct expression.

Slogan, Motto
A **slogan** is a catch phrase used by a political party, fraternity, or other organization in advertising or promotion. A **motto** is a short phrase that usually expresses a moral aim or purpose.

Solid, Stolid
Solid means reliable when referring to a person's character.
*He has a reputation as a **solid** citizen.*

Stolid means unemotional or stoic.
*The funny entertainer could even make a **stolid** person let loose.*

Some body, Somebody
Some body refers to any single person or thing.
*She met with **some body** in administration about her concern.*

Somebody refers to any person.
***Somebody** can talk to the administration about the problem.*

Some day, Someday
Some day refers to a particular day.
*We all hope and pray that **some day** they are back together.*

Someday refers to an indefinite time in the future.
*No doubt, if we stay on this course, we'll succeed **someday**.*

Some time, Sometime, Sometimes
Some time means a period of time.
*Gordon needs **some time** to think over the attractive job offer.*

Sometime refers to an indefinite time in the future.
*Let's try to get together and have lunch **sometime**.*

Sometimes means now and then.
*Tim likes golf a lot, but **sometimes** he needs to give it a rest.*

Somewhere, Somewheres

Somewhere is the correct word.
Somewhere out in deep space, our planet might have a twin.

Son-in-laws, Sons-in-law

Sons-in-law is the correct phrase.

Sordid story, Sorted story

Sordid story is the correct phrase.

Sort of, Kind of

*See entry for **Kind of, Sort of**.*

Southward, Southwards

Southward is preferred in American usage.

Spacious, Specious

Spacious means roomy or large in area.
*The hotel offers **spacious** accommodations at affordable rates.*

Specious means plausible but false.
*He is known for using **specious** arguments to back his claims.*

Spade, Spayed

Spade is a small digging tool.
*The soil in our garden can be turned by hand with a **spade**.*

A **spayed** female animal has had its ovaries removed.
Spayed cats are typically affectionate, calm, and healthy.

Specially, Especially

*See entry for **Especially, Specially**.*

Specie, Species

Concerning classification in biology, **species** is the correct spelling for both singular and plural.
*This (or those) **species** may soon be extinct.*

Spiritual, Spirituous

Spiritual refers to the spirit or soul.
*Friends can offer comfort, empathy, and **spiritual** support.*

Spirituous refers to certain kinds of alcoholic drinks.
*The city allows selling **spirituous** liquors in sealed containers.*

Spontaneous, Impromptu, Extemporaneous

*See entry for **Extemporaneous, Impromptu, Spontaneous**.*

Spoor, Spore

Spoor is the track or trail of an animal.
*The hunters are tracking the deer in the snow by its own **spoor**.*

Spore is the reproductive organ of a fern, algae, and some other plant-like organisms.
*You can see the **spores** under the leaves of the fern.*

Sporadic, Periodic

*See entry for **Periodic, Sporadic**.*

Squash, Quash

*See entry for **Quash, Squash**.*

Stain glass, Stained glass

Stained glass is the correct phrase.

Stalactites, Stalagmites

Both words refer to crystalline deposits of calcium carbonate found in caves. **Stalactites** hang from the ceiling, and **stalagmites** rise from the ground.

Stanch, Staunch

Stanch means to block something.
*They're allocating money to **stanch** the flow of illegal drugs.*

Staunch means dedicated or loyal. It can also mean watertight or sound (*a **staunch** ship*).
*Bob is always a **staunch** supporter of that political party.*

Stanza, Verse

Technically, a **stanza** is a succession of lines that form a poem or a song. **Verse** is a single line of writing. However, we also call a series of lines in a song a **verse**.

Stationary, Stationery

Stationary means unable to move or to stand still.
Stationary bikes offer a great cardio lower-body workout.

Stationery is paper for letter writing.
Creating personalized business stationery is easy.

Statue, Stature, Statute

Statue is a sculpture that represents a human or animal.
With the base and pedestal, the Statue of Liberty is 305 feet tall.

Stature refers to height or status.
The child could have a genetic short stature or a growth delay.
Their software company grew in stature in just a few years.

Statute refers to an established law or rule.
The city's statute of limitations limits the time for tax collection.

Stimulant, Stimulus

Stimulant refers to drugs or other things that increase activity.
Caffeine, a mild stimulant, acts on the central nervous system.

Stimulus refers to an incentive that initiates activity.
Music alone can provide a stimulus to a person's imagination.

Stipend, Honorarium

See entry for Honorarium, Stipend.

Straight, Strait

Straight means not curved.
Unlike many rivers, the Hudson River runs straight for one mile.

Strait, as an adjective, means confined or restricted. As a noun, it means a narrow passage.
He is a pretty strait-laced type of person with high principles.
The Strait of Hormuz is the entrance to the Persian Gulf.

Stratosphere, Atmosphere

The **stratosphere** is the layer of **atmosphere** between 7 and 50 miles up, and the **atmosphere** is the gaseous layer surrounding earth.

Stupid, Ignorant

*See entry for **Ignorant, Stupid**.*

*"A city **statute** prohibits a **statue** of this **stature**,"* the inspector told the sculptor.

Subnormal, Abnormal
*See entry for **Abnormal, Subnormal**.*

Subscribe, Ascribe
*See entry for **Ascribe, Subscribe**.*

Subsequent, Consequent
*See entry for **Consequent, Subsequent**.*

Substantial, Substantive
Substantial means considerable or sizeable.
*We need a **substantial** revenue increase to meet our goals.*

Substantive means actual or firm.
*The boss is taking **substantive** measures to prevent layoffs.*

Supercede, Supersede
The preferred spelling is **supersede**.

Supernatural, Supranatural
Supernatural means not of this world and not explainable by natural laws.
*The discussion centered on aliens, UFOs, and other **supernatural** phenomena.*

Supranatural, a rare word, means contrived, artificial, or inconsistent with prevailing customs.
*After some **supranatural** and paranormal theories, they looked to more scientific hypotheses.*

Supine, Prone, Prostate, Prostrate
*See entry for **Prone, Prostate, Prostrate, Supine**.*

Supplement, Augment
*See entry for **Augment, Supplement**.*

Supposably, Supposedly

Though both words can be found in dictionaries and are close in meaning, the preferred word is **supposedly**.

*They **supposedly** saved the toughest questions for the end.*

Suppose, Supposed

Suppose, a verb, means to think or guess.

Suppose we win the lottery. What are we buying first?

Supposed, an adjective, means accepted as such or believed, but often with a doubtful connotation.

*His **supposed** expertise did not impress the computer programmers who had worked with his software.*

Suppose to, Supposed to

Supposed to is the correct phrase.

*What is **supposed to** be so special about this design software?*

Sure, Surely

Sure is an adjective.

*Waiting for hours is a **sure** sign of his patience and dedication.*

Surely is an adverb.

*Waiting for hours is **surely** a sign of his patience and dedication.*

Note: Careful writers try to avoid using the following informal uses of **sure**:

Sure enough, I'll be there.
*She **sure** is a nice person.*
*He **sure** needed the money.*
Sure, I want to attend college.

Sure and, Sure to

Sure to is the correct phrase.

*Be **sure to** negotiate beneficial compromises for every client.*

Sympathy, Empathy

*See entry for **Empathy, Sympathy**.*

Syntax, Grammar

Syntax is a part of grammar that deals with how words form phrases, clauses, and sentences. **Grammar** is the complete study of a language.

Systematize, Systemize

Systematize is the preferred spelling, but either is acceptable.

T

"Use the right word and not its second cousin."—Mark Twain

T–shirt, Tee shirt
Either spelling is acceptable.

Take, Bring
See entry for **Bring, Take**.

Take a different tack, Take a different tact
Take a different tack is the correct phrase. It means to take a different strategy, and it derives from the nautical term *tack*, which is a ship's direction in relation to the position of its sails. *We are going to **take a different tack** later and focus on quality.*

Tantamount, Paramount
See entry for **Paramount, Tantamount**.

Tartar, Plaque
Tartar (also called dental calculus) is a hard, yellowish **plaque** that collects food particles and salt deposits. **Plaque** is a thin film of mucus and bacteria on a tooth's surface.

Taunt, Taut, Tout
Taunt means to jeer, mock, scoff, or tease someone.
*Ed confronted the person who **taunted** him during his speech.*

Taut means tightly stretched or tense.
*For safety reasons, the rope is kept **taut** for the rock climbers.*

Tout means to promote.
*Bill has been **touted** as a possible mayoral candidate.*

Teach, Learn
See entry for **Learn, Teach**.

Temerity, Timidity

Temerity means daring or recklessness.
*Nick had the **temerity** to ask the film star for another autograph.*

Timidity means fearfulness or hesitancy.
Timidity and shyness are common to many young children.

Temperature, Fever

*A person has a **fever** when his or her **temperature** is higher than 98.6° F.*

Tenant, Tenet

Tenant refers to one who holds the right (or lease) to occupy a place.
*The previous **tenant** of this apartment lived here for 12 years.*

Tenet refers to a rule, belief, or part of a body of doctrine.
*Avoiding pork altogether is a **tenet** of some faiths.*

Tenderhooks, Tenterhooks

Tenterhooks, meaning to be as tense as a *tenter* (a person who stretches canvass), is the correct word.

Tendon, Ligament

A **tendon** is the fibrous tissue that connects the muscle to the bone. A **ligament** is the strong connective tissue that connects bones or cartilage at a joint.

Tepid, Vapid

Tepid means lukewarm or unenthusiastic.
*They used **tepid** water for the baby's bath.*
*The crowd greeted the band with a **tepid** reception.*

Vapid means lacking animation, boring, or dull.
*In the interview, he came across as **vapid** and artificial.*

That there, Them there, These here, This here

Avoid these phrases. Just use *that*, *those*, *these*, or *this*.

That, Which

That is used when the word introduces a clause essential (or restrictive) to the meaning of the sentence. **That** helps identify the information and is not set off by commas.
*This is the Chevy **that** has a new engine.*
*Here is the rule **that** applies in both cases.*

Which is used when the word introduces a clause not essential (or nonrestrictive) to the meaning of the sentence. **Which** helps amplify the information and is set off by commas or dashes.
*My Chevy, **which** runs well, has a new engine.*
*This rule, **which** became effective in 2011, applies to you.*

Memory hook: **That** identifies and **which** amplifies.

Thaw, Unthaw

Thaw is the correct word. The *un* is unnecessary.

Their, There, They're

Their is the possessive of the pronoun *they*; **there** is an adverb or a pronoun referring to a place; **they're** is the contraction of *they are*.
***They're** doing all **their** science homework over **there** tonight.*

Theirself, Theirselves, Themself

No such words exist. Substitute *herself* or *himself* for **theirself** and *themselves* for **theirselves** and **themself**.

Thence, Hence, Whence

*See entry for **Hence, Thence, Whence**.*

Therefor, Therefore

Therefor, a rare word, means for this or for that.
*John will explain what we must do first and the causes **therefor**.*

Therefore means hence or consequently.
*We **therefore** hold that the two-week notice is too short.*

These kind, Those kind

Avoid these phrases because they mix a plural word (*these* or *those*) with a singular word (*kind*). Instead, use *this kind* and *that kind*, or *these kinds* and *those kinds*.

Note that this agreement problem can also occur with the phrases *these sort* and *these type*.

These ones, Those ones

Avoid these phrases. Just use *these* or *those*.

Think, Believe, Feel

See entry for **Believe, Feel, Think***.*

Thrash, Thresh

Thrash means to beat, defeat, or move violently.
In yesterday's ballgame, we **thrashed** *the opposition.*
Some in the yoga class **thrashed** *their arms like windmills.*

Thresh means to separate seeds of grain from husks by beating.
The farm workers **thresh** *the wheat in the fields twice a week.*

Throes, Throws

Throes means severe spasm of pain or a condition of struggling.
We're in the **throes** *of remodeling our house for the first time.*

Throws means propels, hurls, or flings.
The news of the profit loss **throws** *a new light on the investment.*

Through, Thru

Though it is quite common, **thru** is a nonstandard word and should be avoided. Use **through** instead.

Throughfare, Thoroughfare

Thoroughfare, meaning a public road, is the correct word.

Throughway, Thruway

Thruway, meaning an expressway, is the more common word. It is derived from the words *through* and *highway*.

Thus, Thusly

Thusly is a nonstandard word. Avoid its use.

Tidbit, Titbit

Tidbit is preferred in American usage.

Tide me over, Tie me over

Tide me over, which means to help one survive a scarcity of some resource, is the correct expression. The phrase refers to a swelling tide, which can carry a small boat over an obstacle without requiring effort on the boat's part.
*This job will **tide me over** financially until I find a better one.*

Till, Until

Though considered less formal, the word **till** is acceptable shorthand for **until**. Note that 'til, a contraction of **until**, is an old form that has been replaced by **till**.

Timber, Timbre

Timber refers to cut wood and, figuratively, to qualify for a certain position.
*The **timber** company worked on replanting trees all spring.*
*The new trainee has management **timber**.*

Timbre refers to the quality of sound.
*The young choir voices have great range and beautiful **timbre**.*

Tint, Hue, Shade

*See entry for **Hue, Shade, Tint**.*

Titillate, Titivate

Titillate means to stimulate, tickle, or arouse pleasantly.
*The spicy chicken wings always **titillate** our taste buds.*

Titivate means adorn or spruce up.
*Hand-painted murals of famous jazz musicians **titivate** the walls.*

Titled, Entitled

*See entry for **Entitled, Titled**.*

Toe the line, Tow the line

Toe the line, meaning to conform to stated standards, is the correct expression and is equivalent to *toe the mark*. The phrase refers to two things: the starting mark in a foot race (the runners must *toe the line*), and the center line in a boxing ring where boxers stand and go toe to toe.

*Pressure is building on the other companies to **toe the line** on the new environmental regulations.*

Tongue and cheek, Tongue in cheek

Tongue in cheek is the correct phrase (meaning kidding). It derives from the practice of putting one's tongue into one's cheek to keep from laughing at an inappropriate moment.

*Pat wrote a lighthearted, **tongue in cheek** article about his college experiences.*

Tortuous, Torturous

Tortuous means winding or crooked.
*The bus took a **tortuous** route getting to the concert venue.*

Torturous means causing pain.
*The steep mountain path is quite **torturous** to our legs and feet.*

Toward, Towards

Toward is preferred in American usage.

Track home, Tract home

Tract home is the correct phrase. It refers to a mass-produced house that has a common construction method and design.
***Tract homes** continue to be popular in many areas of the town.*

Transient, Transitory

Transient means brief or fleeting (it usually applies to people).
*Mr. Dracon and Mr. Sasnowitz are **transient** guests at this hotel.*

Transitory means **transient** but usually applies to events.
*Do not worry, the noisy circus is **transitory**.*

Translator, Interpreter

A **translator** converts writing to another language, and an **interpreter** converts speech to another language.

Translucent, Transparent, Opaque

*See entry for **Opaque, Translucent, Transparent**.*

Triumphal, Triumphant

Triumphal means to celebrate or to honor a success or victory.
*The baseball team had a **triumphal** celebration in its home city.*

Triumphant means to show a feeling of rejoice for success.
*The crowd greeted the players with **triumphant** shouts of joy.*

Troop, Troupe

Troop is a group of people or animals.
*A **troop** of new students is attending orientation this week.*

Troupe is a company of actors or performers.
*The Ithaca College Trombone **Troupe** was started in 1982.*

*The vaudeville **troupe** entertained the **troops**.*

Trooper, Trouper

A **trooper** is a mounted soldier or police officer, or a state police officer.
*The **trooper** told the new drivers to always wear seatbelts.*

A **trouper** is a member of a group of actors or performers. The idiom, "He's a real trouper" means the person contributes to his team or group.
*John is a real **trouper**—he played today despite a broken arm.*

Trustee, Trusty

Trustee is someone entrusted to manage the property of others.
*Mary Jane is the public guardian and **trustee** of their estate.*

Trusty is a trustworthy prisoner who has special privileges.
*The reliable **trusty** was given a new job in the prison's library.*

Try and, Try to

Try to remember that **try to** is the correct phrase.
*We **try to** negotiate beneficial compromises for all of our clients.*

Tune, Melody

A **tune** is an easily remembered *melody*. A **melody** is a group of notes in a certain order that results in a nice sound.

Turban, Turbine

Turban is a close-fitting hat consisting of material wound around a small inner cap. **Turbine** is a machine with blades or rotors that are driven by the pressure from fluid, steam, or gas.

Turbid, Turgid

Turbid means muddy, opaque, or unclear.
*The large mountain lake appears **turbid** after the heavy rainfall.*

Turgid means swollen or pompous.
*Steve's abdominal area is **turgid** and sensitive from the surgery.*
*The radio personality has a **turgid** style of talking to his guests.*

Turn into, Turn to

Turn into means to transform something.
*Contrary to popular belief, muscles never **turn into** fat.*

Turn to means seek advice or solace from, or to go to a certain page in a book.
*Dissatisfied with his scores, Bill **turned to** his pro for advice.*
*The professor asked the physics class to **turn to** page 12.*

Type, Click, Press

*See entry for **Click, Press, Type**.*

Typhoon, Hurricane

A **typhoon** is a severe tropical storm that starts west of the International Date Line (Pacific Ocean or China Sea). A **hurricane** is a severe tropical storm that starts east of the International Date Line (Atlantic Ocean, Caribbean Sea, or Gulf of Mexico).

Tyrannical yolk, Tyrannical yoke

Tyrannical yoke, meaning a tyrant's aggressive power, is the correct phrase.
*They freed themselves from their leader's **tyrannical yoke**.*

U

"Writers take words seriously—perhaps the last professional class that does."—John Updike

Ulterior, Alterior

Ulterior, as in ***ulterior*** *motive*, is the correct word.

Ultimate, Penultimate

*See entry for **Penultimate, Ultimate**.*

Ultimately, Eventually

*See entry for **Eventually, Ultimately**.*

Unalienable, Inalienable

Either word is correct, but **inalienable** is more common today.

Unaware, Unawares

Unaware is an adjective meaning not being aware of something.
*The organizers are **unaware** of the inclement weather forecast.*

Unawares is an adverb meaning by surprise or unexpectedly.
*The inclement weather caught the picnic organizers **unawares**.*

Unbeknown, Unbeknownst

Either spelling is acceptable.

Unbelievable

This is a much overused word. It actually means *too improbable to believe* rather than its common misuse of *good*.
*The festival offers **good** (not **unbelievable**) apple pies every fall.*
*To them, the UFO story of Roswell, New Mexico is **unbelievable**.*

Uncharted territory, Unchartered territory

Uncharted territory is the correct phrase.

Uncomprehensible, Comprehensive, Comprehensible

See entry for **Comprehensive, Comprehensible, Uncomprehensible.**

Unconscience, Unconscious

Unconscience is not a word.

Under way, Underway

Either spelling is acceptable.

Understated, Unstated

Understated means said in restrained terms or done in a restrained manner.
*The company praised the product but **understated** its deficiencies.*

Unstated means unsaid.
*They followed **unstated** rules of conduct and dress.*

Undo, Undue

Undo means to reverse something.
*It will take much rain to **undo** the damage caused by the drought.*

Undue means inappropriate or excessive.
*They should be quiet and refrain from any **undue** criticism.*

Undoubtably, Undoubtedly

Undoubtably is not a word.

Undoubted, Redoubtable, Indubitable

See entry for **Indubitable, Redoubtable, Undoubted.**

Uneatable, Unedible, Inedible

See entry for **Inedible, Uneatable, Unedible.**

Unequivocably, Unequivocally

Unequivocably is not a word.

Unessential, Nonessential, Inessential

All three of these words are considered synonyms.

Unhealthful, Unhealthy
*See entry for **Healthful, Healthy**.*

Unilateral, Bilateral, Multilateral
*See entry for **Bilateral, Multilateral, Unilateral**.*

Uninterested, Disinterested
*See entry for **Disinterested, Uninterested**.*

United Kingdom, British Isles, Great Britain
*See entry for **British Isles, Great Britain, United Kingdom**.*

University, College
A **university** grants bachelor's, master's, and doctorate degrees.
A **college** mainly grants bachelor's degrees.

Unloosen, Loosen
Loosen is the correct word. The *un* is not needed.

Unorganized, Disorganized
*See entry for **Disorganized, Unorganized**.*

Unprecedented, Rare
*See entry for **Rare, Unprecedented**.*

Unreadable, Illegible
*See entry for **Illegible, Unreadable**.*

Unsatisfied, Dissatisfied
*See entry for **Dissatisfied, Unsatisfied**.*

Unsoluble, Unsolvable
Both words mean not easily solved.
*The corporation continues to have **unsoluble** (or **unsolvable**) quality problems.*

Note: **Unsoluble** can also mean that something is not soluble in liquid.

Unthaw, Thaw
*See entry for **Thaw, Unthaw**.*

Unthinkable, Inconceivable
*See entry for **Inconceivable, Unthinkable**.*

Until, Till
*See entry for **Till, Until**.*

Unused, Disused
*See entry for **Disused, Unused**.*

Unwanted, Unwonted
Unwanted means not wanted.
*Occasionally we experience **unwanted** e-mails and phone calls.*

Unwonted means out of the ordinary or unusual.
*At the party, the children were in an **unwonted** state of excitement when they learned a clown was coming.*

Upmost, Outmost, Utmost
*See entry for **Outmost, Upmost, Utmost**.*

Upward, Upwards
Upward is preferred in American usage.

Urban, Urbane
Urban refers to a city.
*A good example of **urban** sprawl is Las Vegas, Nevada.*

Urbane means polished or smooth, as in a person's demeanor.
*The diplomat's **urbane** and polite manner impresses everyone.*

Use to, Used to
Used to is the correct phrase.
*Up until a year ago, we **used to** watch that TV drama regularly.*

V

"I know many books which have bored their readers, but I know of none which has done real evil."—Voltaire

Vail, Vale, Veil

Vail means to lower as a sign of respect.
*You should **vail** the flag because our former governor just died.*

Vale refers to a valley.
*His walk took him through **vale** country and agricultural land.*

Veil is a face covering or something that conceals or obscures.
*The women wear a black **veil** to hide their faces.*
*Their organization operated under a **veil** of secrecy.*
*They have always **veiled** their undercover activities.*

Valueless, Invaluable

*See entry for **Invaluable, Valueless**.*

Vapid, Tepid

*See entry for **Tepid, Vapid**.*

Varied, Various

Varied is the past tense of *vary*.
*The chef **varied** the salad vegetables according to the season.*

Various means distinct, diverse, or many different kinds.
*The company officers come from **various** backgrounds.*

Vein, Artery

A **vein** carries blood to the heart, and an **artery** carries blood from the heart to other parts of the body.

Venal, Venial

Venal means susceptible to corruption, dishonesty, or bribery.
*The candidate didn't commit the **venal** offense of bribing voters.*

Venial means easily excused or forgiven.
*Eating meat on Fridays was once a **venial** sin to Catholics.*

Veneer, Venire

Veneer is a very thin layer of material or a superficial manner.
*We applied a **veneer** of walnut to the ugly pine table.*
*Their dissatisfaction was disguised by a **veneer** of friendliness.*

Venire is a prospective juror panel from which a jury is selected.
*Ten members of the **venire** received instructions from the court.*

Veracious, Voracious

Veracious means completely truthful or accurate.
*When the **veracious** child speaks, never doubt her honesty.*

Voracious means having an insatiable appetite.
*Since age 10, Tim has been a **voracious** reader of comics.*
*Among children, the demand for chocolate is **voracious**.*

Verbage, Verbiage

Verbiage is the correct word.

Verbal, Oral

*See entry for **Oral, Verbal**.*

Verbiage, Verbosity

Verbiage is excessive wordiness, usually written.
*The contract was padded with too much legal **verbiage**.*

Verbosity is excessive and boring wordiness, usually spoken.
*The guest speaker's **verbosity** almost put the audience to sleep.*

Verse, Stanza

Technically, a **stanza** is a succession of lines that form a poem or a song. **Verse** is a single line of writing. However, we also call a series of lines in a song a **verse**.

Vertebra, Vertebrae

Vertebra is the singular form.
*While grabbing the barbell, I chipped my L4 **vertebra**.*

Vertebrae is the plural form.
*He said my problem was between the C3 and C4 **vertebrae**.*

Vial, Vile

Vial is a small closable container usually for liquids.
*The lab technician put the remaining liquid in a small glass **vial**.*

Vile means despicable, repulsive, or disgustingly bad.
*We experienced **vile** weather during our Alaskan cruise.*

Vice, Vise

Vice refers to a bad habit or wickedness.
*His only **vices** are coffee and loud music.*

Vise is the clamp used in carpentry or metal work.
*To change the grip, clamp the golf club in a **vise**.*

Vicious, Viscose, Viscous

Vicious refers to being savage or cruel.
*The mean dog displayed **vicious** behavior toward the jogger.*

Viscose refers to a thick organic liquid used for making rayon and cellophane.
*The dress uses a 100-percent **viscose** fabric for a light, cool feel.*

Viscous refers to a thick or gummy liquid that is hard to pour.
*Typical **viscous** liquids are molasses, honey, oil, and syrup.*

Vicious circle, Vicious cycle

Vicious circle is the correct phrase.
*Last year she went through a **vicious circle** of changing jobs.*

Vigorish, Vigorous

Vigorish refers to interest or fees paid to a lender.
*Standard **vigorish** charges of 10 percent are figured into the amount due.*

Vigorous means energetic, robust, or strong.
__Vigorous__ exercise can decrease the risk of heart disease.

Vigorous, Rigorous

*See entry for **Rigorous, Vigorous**.*

Villain, Villein

Villain is a bad person.
*Every James Bond film has at least one **villain** for 007 to catch.*

Villein was a feudal serf in medieval Europe.
***Villeins** are frequently mentioned in the Domesday Book.*

Viola, Voila

A **viola** is a flower or a stringed musical instrument. **Voila** is a French expression that means *behold* or *look there.*

*The **vicious** dog lapped up the **viscous** honey.*

Viral, Virile

Viral refers to a virus.
*Some community-acquired pneumonias are **viral** in origin.*

Virile refers to being manly.
*The **virile** athletes work out four hours every day.*

Visa, Passport

A **visa** is an official authorization stamped on a passport that permits a person's entry into and travel within a country. A **passport** is an official government document that certifies a person's identity and citizenship and permits travel to another country.

Visible, Visual

Visible means able to be seen or noticeable.
*The used car he bought had no **visible** flaws or damage.*
*The diet made a **visible** difference in his look.*

Visual refers to sight.
*Many of us will acquire **visual** impairment in later life.*

Vocal chords, Vocal cords

Vocal cords is the correct phrase.

Vocation, Evocation, Avocation

*See entry for **Avocation, Evocation, Vocation**.*

Vouch, Avow

*See entry for **Avow, Vouch**.*

W

"A new word is like a wild animal you have caught. You must learn its ways and break it before you can use it."—H.G. Wells

Waiver, Waver

Waiver, you relinquish a right, privilege, or claim.
*Jim signed a **waiver** of his right to sue for any past-due royalties.*

Waver means to vacillate or be indecisive.
*Kevin says he will not **waver** on the issue of past-due royalties.*

Wane, Wax

Wane means to gradually decrease in strength or size.
*Their enthusiasm for our idea is definitely beginning to **wane**.*

Wax means to increase in size or strength.
*Our interest in the house started to **wax** when we saw the huge kitchen, but it subsided when we saw the moldy basement.*

Wangle, Wrangle

Wangle means to gain by trickery or contrivance.
*He **wangled** a job for which he had no qualifications.*

Wrangle means to argue or debate something angrily.
*The two coaches **wrangled** over the umpire's call.*

Wrangle also means herding or tending saddle horses.
*Paul has been **wrangling** horses in Virginia for many years now.*

Warrantee, Warranty

Warrantee is the person to whom the **warranty** is given.
*The dealer gave the **warrantee** the required forms to complete.*

Warranty is a promise to repair or replace a faulty product.
*Vehicles under a factory **warranty** will be repaired at no charge.*

Wary, Weary

Wary means cautious or watchful.
*She and John are **wary** about replacing their insurance policy.*

Weary means fatigued or tired.
*The players are **weary** after a long week of overtime matches.*

Wean, Ween

Wean means to cause to give up something.
*The doctor is trying to **wean** him from his daily cigarettes.*

Ween means to think, suppose, or imagine something.
*We are asking students to **ween** new ideas for the school play.*

Weather, Wether, Whether

Weather, as a noun, refers to the atmosphere with respect to heat or cold, wetness or dryness, calm or storm, and clearness or cloudiness over a short time period. As a verb, it can also mean to endure or resist.
*The **weather** is too cold to attempt an outdoor run.*
*Some nations will be able to **weather** the financial crisis.*

Note: Unlike the word **weather**, the word *climate* refers to how the atmosphere behaves over a *long time period*.

Wether is a male sheep or ram, or a castrated ram or billy goat.
*A **wether** flock invaded the town unexpectedly and scared many.*

Whether introduces an indirect question, involving implied choices, or presents alternative conditions or possibilities.
*We have great concert seats, **whether** by chance or on purpose.*
*Training is needed **whether** you are an employee or a manager.*

Well, Good

*See entry for **Good, Well**.*

Wench, Winch

Wench is a girl or young woman, often a servant.
*The kitchen **wench** brought the prince his dinner.*

Winch is a device that lifts or pulls heavy objects.
*The tractor was equipped with a **winch** to pull out tree stumps.*

Went, Gone

*See entry for **Gone, Went**.*

We're, Were

We're is a contraction for *we are*.
*To increase our chances, **we're** applying to many good colleges.*

Were is a past tense form of the verb *be*.
*Bill and Tom **were** applying to many colleges on the West Coast.*

Westward, Westwards

Westward is preferred in American usage.

Wet your appetite, Whet your appetite

Whet your appetite (from *whetstone*) is correct. It means to sharpen your appetite.
*I hope the menu selections **whet your appetite**.*

Wheat, Whole-wheat

Prefer the phrase **whole-wheat** in formal writing.
*White **whole-wheat** bread can add whole grains to your diet.*

When and if

Avoid this colloquial expression in formal writing.
*If (not **when and if**) the budget is approved, you will be trained.*

Whence, Thence, Hence

*See entry for **Hence, Thence, Whence**.*

Whereas, although

*See entry for **Although, Whereas**.*

Which, That

*See entry for **That, Which**.*

Whiskey, Whisky

The preferred spelling in the United States and Ireland is **whiskey**. Great Britain and Canada use **whisky**.

Whither, Wither

Whither means to what place.
*"**Whither** thou goest, I will go."* (Ruth 1:16)

Wither means to dry up or shrivel from lack of moisture.
*The plants in the green house **wither** without sufficient water.*

Who, Whom

Though some people today tend to ignore the difference in these words, careful writers and speakers retain this distinction of nominative and objective pronoun case.

To choose the correct pronoun of **who** or **whom**, you need to recognize whether the pronoun is being used as a subject (the nominative form) or an object (the objective form). **Who** is nominative (for subjects), and **whom** is objective (for objects).
***Who** (subject) left the party last?*
***Whom** (object) should the invitation go to?*

Trick example:
*The gift must be returned by **whoever** bought it.*

Here the whole clause ***whoever** bought it* is the object of the preposition *by*. But ***whoever*** remains nominative because it is the subject of that clause.

Another tip is to try substituting a personal pronoun (*he, she, him, her, they, them,* and others) in place of **who** or **whom**. If *he, she,* or *they* fits, use **who**.

Who is the junior senator from that state?
She is the junior senator from that state.

If *him, her,* or *them* fits, use **whom**.
The outcome could depend on **whom**.
The outcome could depend on *them*.

Who's, Whose

Who's is the contraction for *who is*.
***Who's** that person you are recommending for the position?*

Who's can also mean *who has*.
***Who's** been sending money to the charity anonymously?*

Whose is the possessive form of *who*.
***Whose** report card shows the most improvement from last year?*

Will, Shall

*See entry for **Shall, Will**.*

Wimbleton, Wimbledon

Wimbledon is the correct name of the tennis location in England.

Win loss, Won loss

The correct expression is **won-loss**.
*The team had an impressive **won-loss** record last year.*

With regard to, With regards to

With regard to, without an *s*, is the correct phrase. Note that often you can substitute words such as *on*, *about*, or *concerning*.
*He notified us **with regard to** (on, about, concerning) the cost.*

Without further adieu, Without further ado

Without further ado is the correct phrase.
*Now, **without further ado**, here are the answers to the quiz.*

World Wide Web

Like the word *Internet*, the phrase **World Wide Web** is always capitalized.

World-renown, World-renowned

World-renowned is the correct phase.
*The **world-renowned** singer was known for his gifts to charity.*

Worse comes to worse, worst comes to worst

Though illogical, **worst comes to worst** is the correct phrase.
*If **worst comes to worst** you can apply for a refund.*

Would have, Would of

Would have is the correct phrase.
*If you had read the book, you **would have** known the answer.*

Wrack, Rack

Wrack and **rack** both mean to strain or torment. Prefer **rack**.
*We are **racking** our brains to remember the name of that song.*

Wrapped, Rapt

*See entry for **Rapt, Wrapped**.*

Wreak, Wreck

Wreak means to cause something, almost always trouble.
*Unexpected expenses **wreak** havoc on the department budget.*

Wreck means to destroy something.
*Unexpected expenses **wrecked** our organization's budget.*

Wreaking havoc, Reeking havoc

Wreaking havoc is the correct phrase.
*The unusually bad weather is **wreaking havoc** in some states.*

Wreath, Wreathe

Wreath refers to flowers or other things intertwined into a circle.
*Pat and Russ chose a holiday **wreath** for the centerpiece.*

Wreathe means to proceed on a repeatedly curving course.
*The smoke continues to **wreathe** upward through the trees.*

Wretch, Retch

Wretch refers to a pitiable or groveling person. **Retch** refers to vomiting or gagging.

Wright, Right

*See entry for **Right, Wright**.*

Y

"Think like a wise man but communicate in the language of the people."—William Butler Yeats

Yay, Yea, Yeah

Yay or yea means *yes* in an oral vote, hurrah, or to this extent.
*All those in favor of the change, please say **yea**.*
***Yay**! We finally beat the competition.*
*He caught a large catfish about **yea** big.*

Yeah means *yes* in casual speech or writing.
***Yeah**, I'd love to join the school's debating team.*

Yoke, Yolk

Yoke is a crosspiece holding two things together.
*The ox with the plow has a wooden **yoke** around its neck.*

Yolk is the yellow part of an egg.
*The **yolk** of the egg contains most of the protein.*

Yore, Your, You're

Yore is an old word meaning *time long past*.
*The days of **yore** were filled with many courageous heroes.*

Your is the possessive form of *you*.
*The application form is on **your** desk.*

You're is a contraction of *you are*.
*If **you're** interested, they post new job listings every Sunday.*

Young, Youthful

Young means immature or not advanced in age.
*She is looking after his two **young** children, ages 2 and 4.*

Youthful means having attractive qualities of youth.
*Her **youthful** exuberance keeps everyone on their toes.*

Z

"Words are the only tools you've got. Learn to use them with originality and care."—William Zinsser

Zeal, Zest

Zeal refers to a keen interest in pursuing something.
*They were filled with **zeal** to see their favorite band perform.*

Zest refers to keen enjoyment, quality, or flavor.
*His **zest** for life will be missed by all.*
*Having many singers on stage adds **zest** to the play.*
*The wine may contain a dash of pepper for an added **zest**.*

Zealous, Jealous

*See entry for **Jealous, Zealous**.*

Zenith, Nadir

Nadir (lowest point) is the point on the celestial sphere directly below the observer, exactly opposite the **zenith** (highest point).
*They reached a **nadir** of despair when they lost their home.*
*When we adopted our son, we reached the **zenith** in our lives.*

About the Author

Dave Dowling has spent over 30 years in industry as a technical writer, editor, and instructor. His experience includes commercial and government work for large corporations.

Before a career in technical communications, Dave worked in radio syndication in Los Angeles, where he assisted in the production of nationally syndicated radio shows *American Top 40* and *American Country Countdown*. In addition to being a member of the *Society for Technical Communications*, Dave is also the author of *The Dictionary of Worthless Words, Steve Reeves – His Legacy in Films*, and *Images of Steve Reeves*.

The author holds an M.S. from the University at Albany, N.Y. and a B.A. from the State University College at Potsdam, N.Y. He currently lives in Saratoga Springs, New York.

Bibliography

Writing Guides

The following *excellent* writing books were consulted in preparing this book:

The Careful Writer: A Modern Guide to English Usage, Theodore M. Bernstein. New York: Atheneum, 1977.

College English and Communication, Marie M. Stewart and Kenneth Zimmer. 4th ed. New York: McGraw-Hill, 1982.

The Columbia Guide to Standard American English, Kenneth G. Wilson. New York: Columbia University Press, 1993.

The Dictionary of Disagreeable English, Robert Hartwell Fiske. Cinn, OH: Writer's Digest Books, 2004.

The Elements of Style, William Strunk Jr., and E.B. White. 3rd ed. New York: Macmillan, 1979.

Good Grammar Made Easy, Martin Steinmann and Michael Keller. New York: Gramercy Books, 1999.

The Handbook of Good English, Edward D. Johnson. New York: Facts On File Publications, 1982.

Handbook for Writers, Celia Millward. New York: Holt, Rinehart and Winston, 1983.

Harbrace College Handbook, John C. Hodges, Mary E. Whittens, Winifred B. Horner, Suzanne S. Webb, Robert K. Miller. 11th ed. New York: Harcourt Brace Jovanovich, Publishers, 1990.

The Little, Brown Handbook, H. Ramsey Fowler. Boston: Little, Brown and Company, 1980.

The Office Guide to Modern English Usage, Carol M. Barnum and Jean C. Vermes. 2nd ed. New York: MJF Books, 1991.

Put It in Writing!, Albert Joseph. New and Updated Edition. New York: McGraw-Hill, 1998.

The Random House Handbook, Frederick Crews. 3rd ed. New York: Random House, 1980.

Bibliography

Sleeping Dogs Don't Lay, Richard Lederer and Richard Dowis. New York: St. Martin's Press, 1999.

Strictly Speaking, Edwin Newman. New York: Warner Books, 1974.

Woe Is I, Patricia T. O'Conner. New York: Riverhead Books, August 1998.

The Wordwatcher's Guide to Good Writing & Grammar, Morton S. Freeman. Cincinnati: Writer's Digest Books, 1990.

The Write Way, Richard Lederer and Richard Dowis. New York: Pocket Books, 1995.

The Writer's Art, James J. Kilpatrick. Kansas City: Andrews and McMeel, June 1993.

Dictionaries and Style Guides

The following *excellent* dictionaries and style guides were consulted in preparing this book:

American Century Dictionary. New York: Reissue. Warner Books, Incorporated, 1996.

American Heritage Dictionary of the English Language. 4th ed. New York: Houghton Mifflin Company, 2010.

Associated Press Stylebook and Libel Manual. Revised and Updated Edition. 43rd ed. New York: Basic Books, 2009.

Chicago Manual of Style. 16th ed. Chicago: Univ. of Chicago Press, 2010.

Merriam-Webster's Collegiate Dictionary. 11th ed. Springfield, MA: Merriam-Webster, 2008.

Oxford American Desk Dictionary and Thesaurus. 3rd ed. New York: Berkley Publishing Group, 2010.

Random House Webster's College Dictionary. 3rd ed. New York: Random House, 2000

Random House Webster's Unabridged Dictionary. 2nd ed. New York: Random House, 2005

Webster's New World College Dictionary. 4th ed. New York: Wiley, John & Sons, Inc., 2004.

Webster's New World Roget's Thesaurus A-Z. 4th ed. New York: Wiley, John & Sons, Inc., 1999.

Also from Marion Street Press

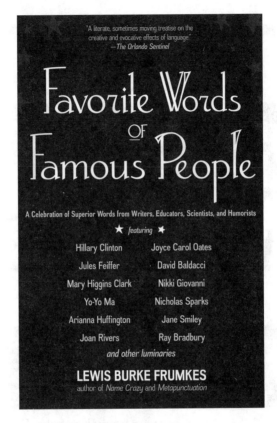

"A literate, sometimes moving treatise on the creative and evocative effects of language."
— The Orlando Sentinel

Favorite Words
OF
Famous People

A Celebration of Superior Words from Writers, Educators, Scientists, and Humorists

★ featuring ★

Hillary Clinton	Joyce Carol Oates
Jules Feiffer	David Baldacci
Mary Higgins Clark	Nikki Giovanni
Yo-Yo Ma	Nicholas Sparks
Arianna Huffington	Jane Smiley
Joan Rivers	Ray Bradbury

and other luminaries

LEWIS BURKE FRUMKES
author of *Name Crazy* and *Metapunctuation*

"Pretty darned revealing!"
— *Self Magazine*

The favorite words of 250 of the best and brightest contemporary thinkers and creators are collected in this volume that no self-respecting word lover should be without. This cornucopia of words is a frequently funny and often surprisingly intimate and moving look into personality and language.

Reference, Humor
168 pages, Trade Paper, 6 x 9
$12.95 (CAN $13.95)
ISBN 9781933338903

Order: 800.888.4741
www.marionstreetpress.com

Also from Marion Street Press

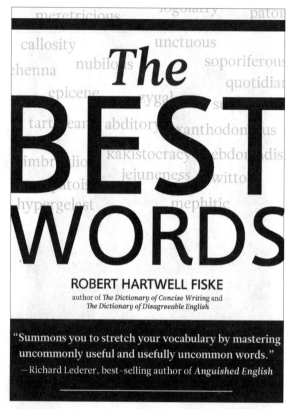

The Best Words

ROBERT HARTWELL FISKE
author of *The Dictionary of Concise Writing* and
The Dictionary of Disagreeable English

"Summons you to stretch your vocabulary by mastering uncommonly useful and usefully uncommon words."
—Richard Lederer, best-selling author of *Anguished English*

"Will definitely be on my best-of-the-word-books bookshelf."
—Mim Harrison, author, *Smart Words* and *Wicked Good Words*

Highlighting the cream of the crop in the English language, this compilation showcases more than 200 exceptional words. Underscoring select terms for their definitions, pronunciations, or both, this exploration resurrects a medley of overlooked examples while also providing instances of their uses in contemporary speech.

Reference, Writing
192 pages, Trade Paper, 5.5 x 8.5
$14.95 (CAN $13.95)
ISBN 9781933338828

Order: 800.888.4741
www.marionstreetpress.com